LIFE LESSONS *from* LITERATURE

LIFE LESSONS
from LITERATURE

Wisdom from
100 Classic Works

JOSEPH PIERCY

Michael O'Mara Books Limited

First published in Great Britain in 2023 by
Michael O'Mara Books Limited
9 Lion Yard
Tremadoc Road
London SW4 7NQ

A CIP catalogue record for this book is available from
the British Library.

This product is made of material from well-managed, FSC®-certified
forests and other controlled sources. The manufacturing processes
conform to the environmental regulations of the country of origin.

ISBN: 978-1-78929-552-8 in hardback print format
ISBN: 978-1-78929-553-5 in ebook format

1 2 3 4 5 6 7 8 9 10

Cover design by Natasha le Coultre, using an illustration
from Shutterstock
Designed and typeset by Ed Pickford
Printed and bound by CPI Group (UK) Ltd, Croydon, CR0 4YY

www.mombooks.com

In loving memory of Dr Alan Piercy

(13 March 1941 – 9 January 2023)

ACKNOWLEDGEMENTS

I would like to thank the following people and places whose help and support has been invaluable in producing this book. My editor at Michael O'Mara Books, Louise Dixon, for her patience and support and inviting me on board with the project. Meredith MacArdle for sifting through my rambling prose. Cover designer Natasha le Coultre and text designer Ed Pickford for their elegant presentation skills. R Lucas and the staff at The University of Sussex library for providing access to thousands of books. And, finally, all the libraries, librarians, bookstores and booksellers, writers and publishers and anyone involved in protecting the sanctity of the printed word around the world, Godspeed to you all.

CONTENTS

INTRODUCTION....1

1 LOVE AND RELATIONSHIPS.....7

2 PEOPLE AND SOCIETY.....35

3 OPPRESSION AND CONFLICT.....88

4 PSYCHOLOGY AND IDENTITY......123

5 HISTORY AND MEMORY.....157

INDEX OF AUTHORS....183

INDEX OF WORKS....184

INTRODUCTION

CONFESSIONS OF A BIBLIOPHILE

I have been trying to remember what was the first book I ever read. By first book, I mean first proper book, first 'grown up' book, the first novel of over two hundred pages. I read, or rather devoured, Roald Dahl books and the Agaton Sax series of detective novels by Swedish children's author Nils-Olof Franzén, among other popular children's classics, but what was the first book that really stayed with me, had a lasting impression and taught me something about life and the world? I think it was *Watership Down* (1972) by Richard Adams, ostensibly a novel about rabbits but also a religious and political allegory that borrows from heroic mythology and the timeless narrative of the flight to freedom and fight against oppression and tyranny. It was also an early example of an eco-thriller. The book is over four hundred pages long and I can remember feeling a sense of achievement when I turned over the last page, but also feeling a curious sense of loss. So engrossed had I been in the story I had come to regard the characters as my friends, and hankered for more. I was missing them already. Nearly twenty-five years passed before Richard Adams wrote a sequel to *Watership Down* but I'd moved on by then, although the rabbits of *Watership Down* will always have a place in my heart and mind.

The great Russian/American novelist Vladimir Nabokov asserted in his famous essay *Good Readers and Good Writers* that 'one cannot read a book: one can only reread it'. I wonder what I would make of *Watership Down* if I was to reread it now? The story that enthralled my eight-year-old imagination is unlikely to have such a profound effect on my tiring, fifty-something mind. Nonetheless, I suspect I would see things that I undoubtedly missed first time round, which is natural given my limited experience of the world when I first read the book. I think the book would fail the Bechdel test regarding the representation of female rabbits in the story. A not uncommon criticism of Adams' novel is that the female rabbits are presented as largely valued only for reproductive purposes (although, in fairness we are talking about rabbits here, who tend to reproduce a lot). Not wishing to sully my fond memories of *Watership Down*. I defied Nabokov's maxim and declined to reread it, thereby leaving the tales of Hazel, Fiver, Bigwig and General Woundwort forever viewed through the lens of my childhood imagination.

I did, however, apply Nabokov's maxim when researching this book, and revisited novels which I had previously read at different stages of my life and different periods of my intellectual development. What was interesting was how differently I feel now about certain books on reacquainting myself with characters and narratives, some of which I read and studied over three decades ago. Nabokov argues that the physical act of reading, of the eye moving across the page and the brain processing the words, means that certain artistic details and nuances that provide depth to a novel are often missed on a first reading. This is a matter for some debate, as it is surely to some degree dependent upon how closely an individual engages with the text and for what purpose. I will concede, however, that Nabokov is right about rereading in terms of missing nuances, but I suggest this may be down to how an individual's view of the world and society may have changed over time. Take, for example, *Slaughterhouse-Five* by Kurt Vonnegut, which I first read as a university undergraduate in my early twenties. I enjoyed the novel; it informed me about the allied bombing of Dresden of which hitherto I had been unaware (winners in a conflict are rarely accused of war crimes), it made me laugh and I revelled in its hallucinatory, scattergun, time-travelling, sci-fi psychedelia. Rereading the novel thirty years later I was struck with how angry the book is and how it is steeped in a disquieting melancholy. Certainly there are jokes in the novel, but they are sad jokes and gallows humour, not the wild dark irreverence I remembered.

Similarly, I studied E.M. Forster at university and found his books crushingly dull. The supposedly comic elements seemed to be so mannered and forced and I cared little for the supposed critique of Edwardian values or the push back against modernity. There is something to be said for the difference between reading for pleasure and reading to write an essay or undertake an exam, so it is possible my view of Forster was coloured by the toil of study. However, rereading *A Room with a View* three decades later, I was struck by how beautifully subtle the irony is, the light and gentle humour and the economy of style, all of which passed me by first time around.

This book is an homage to the joys of reading (or rereading) and aims to highlight how we can enrich our understanding of the world and life through engaging with classical works of literature. The 'life lessons' are not prescriptive; different people read and take different things from different books and interpret themes and ideas in different ways. What I have tried to do is provide a flavour and a few reflections on what can be expected from the different novels on the list. A word about spoilers: I have tried where possible not to give away the entire plots of novels, but at times it was impossible to extrapolate on how a certain theme or moral lesson is illustrated without recourse to key events in the narrative. These entries are merely meant as tasters; there are myriad other delights and interpretations still to be unearthed.

The book is divided into five chapters describing thematic aspects that novels have historically addressed. By far the largest section is the chapter on *People and Society*, but this is naturally because novels are inhabited by characters with human personalities (unless they happen to be talking rabbits), and the traditional view of the novel is that it holds a mirror up to society. The other four chapters also deal with novels about people and society but in narrower or more focused ways, analysing psychology or depicting conflicts. Of course, a case could be made for fitting several novels into multiple sections. *Tess of the d'Urbervilles*, for example, is in the chapter on love and relationships, but it could just as easily be in conflict and oppression or people and society. It is a matter of point of view or highlighting a particular thematic element in the work.

The list of works was compiled with a view to having an international diversity that reflects different cultures. There is an unconscious bias towards European novels, mainly because the novel in its modern form originated and developed in Europe. I have, however, greatly enjoyed discovering books I was not previously familiar with, particularly novels from Asia. The list is largely arbitrary – as all lists of this type are – and makes no pretence to be in any way authoritative and set in stone. What is interesting, however, is that some cursory research of other lists of '100 Greatest Novels of the English language' or '100 Greatest Novels of the Twentieth Century' on the internet brings up many of the same novels as highlighted here, suggesting a level of critical consensus about certain 'classic' works. If I have one regret it is that female writers are rather sparsely represented, although this is indicative of the opportunities afforded to female writers historically. This is changing, however, with recent statistics showing that 70 per cent of the top thousand bestselling novels in the US in 2022 were written by women. If a book similar to this one is produced in a hundred years' time it will most probably have a much more balanced ratio between the genders, or so it is to be hoped.

One of the pleasures of compiling this book has been that it has reignited my love of reading books. It is too easy to become distracted by smartphones, computers, multimedia, the internet, the twenty-four-hour news cycle, streaming television services, etc., and not find the time to sit down in quiet contemplation, pick up a book and read. I have resolved to make that time from now on and cut down on rotting my brain watching memes of skateboarding cats. Books teach us lessons about life, the world around us and the people that inhabit it, and those lessons enrich our understanding of ourselves and others.

Joseph Piercy

CHAPTER 1

LOVE AND RELATIONSHIPS

The exploration of love as a theme has a rich history in the annals of world literature. The romance novel as a genre dates back to the classical Greek romances of the fourth and fifth centuries which established the narrative of an all-consuming passion between protagonists who have to overcome multiple trials and obstacles before they can consummate their love. One notable example of the genre is *Aethiopica* by Heliodorus of Emesa, first translated into European languages in the mid-sixteenth century, which became the model for many writers such as Miguel de Cervantes, William Shakespeare and the seventeenth-century French dramatist Jean-Baptiste Racine, who cited it as his favourite book.

By the nineteenth century, the romantic novel had evolved into an established literary form, and also began portraying women's individuality and desires in a more constructive and positive light. The work of English novelists such as Jane Austen and the Brontë sisters were instrumental in this shift towards the psychology of love and desire. Love as a theme is explored in literature from many different perspectives, be it doomed, tragic love, of which Shakespeare's 'star-crossed lovers' *Romeo and Juliet* is the most famous example, or the romantic comedies of modern-day popular women's fiction. Love is also explored in novels of a darker psychological hue, where obsessive love becomes a destructive force. From whatever angle a writer places love as a central theme, we can learn much about ourselves and our attitudes to, and understanding of, love through fiction.

JANE EYRE BY CHARLOTTE BRONTË

SYNOPSIS

A Gothic romance following the moral
and spiritual development of its strong-
willed eponymous heroine.

LIFE LESSON

Fulfilment in life comes from finding love
that is rooted in moral and spiritual certitude.
It is important to stick to your principles
no matter what life throws at you.

Jane Eyre (1847) is the quintessential novel of the nineteenth-century Gothic romance genre. Populated by cruel grotesques, featuring foreboding and austere settings and signature dark secrets (the classic 'mad woman in the attic'), Charlotte Brontë weaves all the classic Gothic elements into one of the first iconic feminist novels. Although the subject of gender equality is not directly addressed, Jane is strong-willed, independently minded and principled, and shows great fortitude in the face of hardship and misfortune. By the end of the novel Jane has acquired financial independence and status that affords her the luxury of marrying Rochester on her own terms, not on his or those of the patriarchal strictures of mid-Victorian England. Her independence of mind and spirit is beautifully encapsulated in the following quotation:

'I can live alone, if self-respect, and circumstances require me so to do. I need not sell my soul to buy bliss. I have an inward treasure born with me, which can keep me alive if all extraneous delights should be withheld, or offered only at a price I cannot afford to give.'

MADAME BOVARY
BY GUSTAVE FLAUBERT

SYNOPSIS

A dull, undistinguished, provincial French doctor marries an attractive but flighty younger woman who yearns for romantic adventures, intrigues and 'a beautiful life'. In an attempt to escape from the dreary realities of rural living, Emma Bovary embarks upon two doomed affairs.

LIFE LESSON

The inability to distinguish romanticized fantasy from the reality of everyday life can lead to tragedy and ruin.

The titular character of Emma Bovary is a tragic heroine in the classical sense in that she is ultimately undone by all that is false in her. It is easy to regard Emma as capricious and stupid, her head filled with the shallowness of romantic fantasies and dreams. Certainly, Flaubert has fun at Emma's expense with histrionic lines such as: 'She wanted to die but she also wanted to live in Paris.' Her cravings for social status and material wealth are set against the dreariness and customs of country life, hence the novel's original subtitle of 'Provincial Manners'.

Despite her best endeavours and schemes, Emma Bovary remains unfulfilled, as her dreams and fantasies of a 'beautiful life' have distorted her view of reality, or at least the reality of the life expected of her. This disparity between her idealized reveries and the numbing mundanities of Emma's life causes considerable sorrow and frustration, as the following passage encapsulates:

'Deep down, all the while, she was waiting for something to happen. Like a shipwrecked sailor, she kept casting desperate glances over the solitude of her life, seeking some white sail in the distant mists of the horizon. She had no idea by what wind it would reach her, toward what shore it would bear her, or what kind of craft it would *be – tiny boat or towering vessel, laden with heartbreaks or filled to the portholes with rapture. But every morning when she awoke she hoped that today would be the day; she listened for every sound, gave sudden starts, was surprised when nothing happened; and then, sadder with each succeeding sunset, she longed for tomorrow.'*

Flaubert: Corruptor of Public Morals?

Madame Bovary caused a sensation in 1856 when it first appeared as a serial in the literary magazine *Revue De Paris*. Flaubert was tried and acquitted of charges of obscenity and 'corrupting public morality', with the surrounding publicity contributing greatly to sales of the book and to the writer's reputation. Public prosecutors were concerned that the book appeared to glorify adultery among the French middle classes and portrayed a provincial housewife as a proto-nymphomaniac. This is nonsense, of course, and the novel is considered to be one of the masterpieces of nineteenth-century European realist fiction with its elucidation of a particular malaise of the bourgeoisie. Ironically, at the trial the chief prosecutor also argued that any attempt to present reality in fiction should be considered an offence against common decency. It is precisely these hypocritical attitudes of the emergent middle class that the book subtly satirizes.

LOVE IN THE TIME OF CHOLERA BY GABRIEL GARCIA MARQUEZ

SYNOPSIS

The story of a forbidden love affair set against a tumultuous backdrop of wars and disease that spans half a century.

LIFE LESSON

Lovesickness can be considered to be a form of disease, yet one that perseverance and endurance can ultimately overcome and defeat.

This is far from a conventional, sentimental love story. Marquez plays constant tricks on the reader's expectations – an example of this occurs when one of the principal characters is abruptly killed in an accident.

When his love for Fermina is unrequited, Florentino still vows fidelity to her. However, he then embarks upon almost incessant womanizing, seducing and having affairs with hundreds of women. Many of the women he seduces are unhappy and vulnerable, but Florentino shows little sense of responsibility or remorse for his actions, even when the consequences of his seductions result in suicide and murder.

Published in 1985, the novel explores the concept of love from different perspectives and through different social and historical settings. Love eventually transcends multiple hardships and tragedies, although it is not void of deceits and self-deceptions. When Florentino confesses his enduring love for Fermina at her husband's funeral by proclaiming, 'I have waited for this opportunity for more than half a century, to repeat to you once again my vow of eternal fidelity and everlasting love,' he is inviting the reader to be seduced by the narrative of his love.

Did You Know?

The Spanish word for cholera is *cólera*, which has a dual meaning. As well as the disease that provides the background setting for the novel, *cólera* can also mean passionate anger. The title is therefore a pun, combining the sickness of love with its incumbent passions and rage. Perhaps Doctor Juvenal Urbina's commitment to free the city from the ravages of cholera is also a metaphor for freeing his wife Fermina from the rages of her youthful passion for Florentino.

LOLITA BY VLADIMIR NABOKOV

SYNOPSIS

The story of an educated middle-aged man's all-consuming desire for a twelve-year-old girl and its devastating consequences.

LIFE LESSON

Child molesters manipulate, coerce and deceive everything and everyone around them yet remain blithely ignorant of their own moral depravity and cruelty.

Published in 1955, this is Russian émigré writer Vladimir Nabokov's most famous novel and certainly his most controversial. It takes the form of a first-person confessional account of one man's obsessive love of his twelve-year-old stepdaughter, Lolita. Humbert Humbert is no ordinary paedophile, however. Sophisticated, handsome, charming and witty, he recounts his tortuous lust for the object of his affections in hauntingly beautiful prose.

So heart-wrenching are Humbert's angst-filled descriptions, that, combined with his keen eye for detail, clever wordplay and irony, the reader (whom Humbert regularly directly addresses as a member of an imaginary jury) can be forgiven for being seduced into believing his pleas for clemency and understanding.

Nabokov constantly plays tricks on the reader and effects magician-like sleights of hand. Sympathy for Humbert begins to fade once he has consummated his lust for Lolita, and, as the novel progresses, the true extent of his remorseless manipulation and control of Lolita become apparent. Humbert is a highly unreliable narrator and the reader is denied any insight into Lolita's inner world or thoughts, instead being presented with shallow self-justifications. Towards the end, disgust for this monstrous man turns again to a sense of almost pity at how pathetic a figure Humbert has become, hollowed out and destroyed by his obsession and actions, as if he is not even worth the reader's moral revulsion.

A stunning novel that operates on many different levels and is richly inventive, the prose is among the most beautiful written in English. The book is not without its critics, however, uncomfortable with Nabokov's gleeful tricks and wordplay around a subject so darkly shameful. The life lesson above is a fairly obvious and self-evident one, but there are more complex lessons to learn from *Lolita* concerning the nature of human cruelty and indifference to the suffering of others. It is a novel that, once read, demands to be read again as there are many clues, word puzzles and references hidden in the text which are easily missed first time around, but which reward closer inspection.

Pride and Prejudice
by Jane Austen

Synopsis

The story of the stormy relationship
between the daughter of a provincial
squire and a wealthy aristocrat.

Life Lesson

The stubborn sins of pride and prejudice
can jeopardize the chance of happiness
and fulfilment of the heart's desires.

Pride and Prejudice (1813) is the best known and loved of Jane
Austen's novels. The story concerns the relationship between
Elizabeth Bennet, the feisty daughter of a landed gentleman,
and Mr Darcy, a wealthy but aloof aristocrat. At first hostile
to each other, their mutual attraction grows, much against
their initial instincts. The 'will they, won't they?' turbulent
course of the central relationship is played out against
parallel romances of the other Bennet sisters, some of whom
are depicted as frivolous and shallow. Although initially
dismissive of Elizabeth, Darcy comes to appreciate her wit
and intelligence but is resistant through a sense of prejudice
that Elizabeth is below his social standing. Similarly, insulted
by Darcy when they first encounter each other, Elizabeth's
pride is hurt and she struggles to overcome her distrust of

Darcy's aloofness and sense of moral superiority, interpreting it as coldness and cruelty.

Austen explores the manners and attitudes of her time through themes of wealth, marriage and social status. The tone of the novel is foreshadowed in the famous opening line: 'It is a truth universally acknowledged that a single man in possession of a good fortune, must be in want of a wife.' The irony, of course, is that it is the financially troubled Bennet family and the marriage-obsessed Mrs Bennet who are motivated by this supposed 'universal truth'. The opening statement is therefore the inverse of the narrative itself, for it is the Bennet girls' search for a good fortune – or at least financial security – that is the central conceit. In the end Elizabeth refuses to marry for security by rejecting Mr Collins, and only agrees to marry Darcy when she is sure that she truly loves him and he loves her. This, Austen says, is a truly stable basis for marriage.

Pride and Prejudice has been adapted for stage and television many times and in many hybrid forms, cementing its status as the ultimate romantic comedy.

WUTHERING HEIGHTS
BY EMILY BRONTË

SYNOPSIS
Classic Victorian Gothic novel concerning the lives of two families living on the Yorkshire moors and the tempestuous relationships between them.

LIFE LESSON

In matters of the heart people often fail to see what is best for them. Money cannot buy happiness, and vengeance does not conquer torment and pain.

This 1847 novel tells the tale of two landowning families and the intrigues and feuds between the different family members. At the centre is Heathcliff, a foundling who develops a deep and passionate love for his adopted sister Catherine. Although they are not connected by blood, there are practical, financial and social barriers blocking them from consummating their love. Abused and humiliated after the death of his adoptive father, Heathcliff flees the house, Wuthering Heights, only to return a wealthy gentleman and wreak revenge on those who wronged him.

All of the principal characters make wrong decisions which have repercussions for their lives and future happiness. Heathcliff has his revenge and becomes master of Wuthering Heights, but this does not bring him happiness, and he dies bitter and tormented. One recurring theme is characters acting in bad faith. Catherine marries Edgar Linton for palpably the wrong reasons (money and social status) and this starts a train of events leading to tragedy. Similarly, Isabella and Heathcliff's marriage is also undertaken in bad faith and precipitates only misery and cruelty.

Love is a central theme in *Wuthering Heights*, but Brontë presents love in a number of different ways: domestic, maternal, religious, spiritual and obsessive forms of love are all examined. The novel was controversial when it was first published for its representation of domestic cruelty and its challenges to Victorian values and taboos.

ANNA KARENINA BY LEO TOLSTOY

SYNOPSIS

Masterwork of nineteenth-century Russian literature detailing the extramarital affair of a Russian noblewoman with a dashing cavalry officer that scandalizes St Petersburg's social elite.

LIFE LESSON

Romantic love can blind individuals to the realities of life, and love can be a blessing as well as a curse.

'All happy families are alike; each unhappy family is unhappy in its own way' is the famous opening line of this novel. Tolstoy is observing that happy families do not provide a basis for a good story or drama in the way that unhappy families do. The desperately unhappy Anna Karenina imagines herself partaking in the action of the novels she reads. This foreshadows the illusion of romantic love she pursues when she falls uncontrollably in love with Vronsky. For Anna believes she has no choice; she deludes herself that the all-consuming love she feels is somehow meant to be.

The trials and tribulations of Anna and Vronsky's affair is contrasted with the relationship between Kitty and Levin, which is noticeably more prosaic. However, Levin and Kitty work hard at their love and, through mutual respect, forge a partnership which endures and blossoms.

Anna Karenina is more than just a novel about love. Tolstoy weaves in themes of hypocrisy and jealousy, religious faith, fidelity, family loyalties and the institution of marriage. The novel is also set against the backdrop of a period of significant change in Russian society following the abolition of serfdom (of which Tolstoy was a passionate opponent). Tolstoy draws a contrast between the agrarian lifestyles of the emancipated peasants and the high society and fast lifestyles of the city dwellers with their gossip, manners and hypocrisy.

Published in 1878, this a difficult book to read and a long novel at almost nine hundred pages, but alongside Tolstoy's other epic, *War and Peace* (1869), it presents a vivid kaleidoscope of Russian society in the nineteenth century. It remains of equal interest to sociologists and historians as it does to lovers of literature.

THE SORROWS OF YOUNG WERTHER BY JOHANN WOLFGANG VON GOETHE

SYNOPSIS

A hopelessly romantic and idealistic young man falls catastrophically in love with a beautiful young woman betrothed to another man and sinks into a state of intolerable melancholy.

LIFE LESSON

Unrequited love can become unbearable,
but it is crazy to obsess about unattainable
ideals in life, love, nature and art.

Published in 1774, *The Sorrows of Young Werther* is considered
to be the first major novel of *Sturm und Drang* ('Storm and
Stress'), a loose artistic movement in late eighteenth-century
Germany that was an influence on and precursor to European
Romanticism. *Sturm und Drang* writers promoted subjectivity
and explored extreme emotional responses, believing that the
rationalism of the Enlightenment period was stifling the ability
of the arts to reflect the human condition.

Goethe's book is an epistolary novel of letters written by the
titular character to his friend Wilhelm describing his travels
and his obsession with a young, virtuous woman named
Charlotte. Werther is a sensitive soul, already damaged by a
previous unhappy romantic intrigue, when he happens upon
an idyllic small town. Werther is entranced, immersing himself
in the beauty of the surrounding landscape and idealizing the
simple, agrarian life of the local peasants. He then meets and
falls tragically in love with Charlotte, despite knowing she can
never return his ardour.

Goethe's heartbreaking portrait of a young man in turmoil
provided a blueprint for future anti-heroes of the Romantic
movement in European literature. To modern readers,
however, *The Sorrows of Young Werther* can be read as a novel
about anxiety and depression in young adults as they try to
find their own sense and purpose in life.

Did You Know?

Goethe first published the novel anonymously due to some not very well disguised auto-biographical elements in the story. The book quickly developed a cult following (Napoleon Bonaparte was an admirer) which led to a fashion phenomenon known as 'Wertherism'. Fans who identified with the tragic, romantic hero would dress up in the same clothes Werther describes wearing, and parade around holding a copy of the book. There were also reports - largely unsubstantiated - of followers of 'Wertherism' carrying out copycat suicides. The authorities in several European countries were sufficiently concerned about the novel's corruptive influence upon youth to ban it for several decades.

LES LIAISONS DANGEREUSES BY PIERRE CHODERLOS DE LACLOS

SYNOPSIS

Two morally bankrupt aristocrats set about wilfully disrupting and destroying the lives of others through seduction, deception and betrayal.

LIFE LESSON

When people of wealth and privilege have everything they desire, the only commodity that has any value to them is desire itself.

This epistolary novel, published in 1782, recounts the scandalous deeds of two eighteenth-century aristocrats, the Marquise de Merteuil and her former lover the Vicomte de Valmont. The Marquise is smarting after being abandoned by her most recent lover in favour of marriage to a much younger woman, Cécile, and so tries to enlist Valmont to seduce Cécile so she is corrupted before her wedding. Valmont, however, has other plans, and is set on seducing the virtuous and seemingly unattainable wife of a wealthy lawyer. Intrigues, clandestine meetings, seductions and betrayals escalate with devastating consequences for all involved.

Les Liaisons dangereuses paints a devastating picture of the decadence and moral depravity of the French aristocracy in the years leading up to the French Revolution. Merteuil and Valmont have nothing except perpetual leisure, and to relieve their boredom they manipulate and disrupt the lives of other people purely for their own titillation and entertainment. The more virtuous, pure and seemingly unattainable their targets appear, the more they desire to control and corrupt them.

Although some critics have tried to place the novel as a political attack on the Ancien Régime, the French feudal system abolished by the revolution, Laclos enjoyed the patronage of some of the most prominent aristocrats in France. It seems likely then that Laclos' intentions were merely to cause a sensation and to entertain rather than stoke revolutionary fervour. The novel is considered one of the masterworks of pre-revolutionary French literature and its timeless tale of destructive desire, malice and revenge has inspired successful adaptations on stage and screen.

WOMEN IN LOVE
BY D.H. LAWRENCE

SYNOPSIS

A brutal examination of relationships between men and women following two headstrong sisters as they embark upon relationships with two emotionally complex men that prove to be fraught with passion and conflict.

LIFE LESSON

Social values can have a stifling
influence upon instinctive desire and
can bring about sexual repression.

A sequel to D.H. Lawrence's previous novel *The Rainbow* (1915), *Women in Love* continues the story of the Brangwen sisters Ursula, a schoolteacher, and Gudrun, an artist. Both are fiercely independent and strong-minded and have rejected what they see as the conventional role of women in society and the traditional institution of marriage.

The sisters meet two men, Rupert Birkin and Gerald Crich and embark upon relationships with them which are fraught with emotional turmoil. While Rupert's relationship with Ursula develops along a more or less conventional path on the surface, beneath, Rupert is repressing strong desires for Gerald, and his proposal of marriage is an attempt to transfer this desire to Ursula. Gudrun and Gerald's relationship rapidly descends into a cycle of conflict and abuse that threatens to destroy them both.

Women in Love presents a bleak, almost nihilistic view of love, relationships and desire, with constant triangles of conflict causing friction between the main characters. Lawrence wrote the novel during the First World War and although it is seemingly set before the outbreak of war, the sense of impending death and oblivion is prevalent throughout.

The Rainbow and *Women in Love* were initially conceived as one complete novel, but on the advice of Lawrence's publisher the story was split and reworked into two separate volumes. *The Rainbow* was banned from sale in the UK for eleven years on the grounds of obscenity, so its sequel was published first in the United States for a subscriber-only private book club in 1920. It was published in the UK the following year and also received criticism for its graphic depiction of sexuality. It is now acknowledged as a modernist masterpiece.

TESS OF THE D'URBERVILLES
BY THOMAS HARDY

SYNOPSIS

A poor peasant girl suffers a series of social
and moral injustices and abuse at the hands
of a harsh and unforgiving society.

LIFE LESSON

Victorian notions of morality could be deeply
hypocritical, especially the condemnation of
women thought to be sinful and impure.

This 1891 book is a tragic tale of an impoverished and innocent farm girl who is sent to work at the house of a wealthy distant relative. There Tess encounters the heir to the d'Urberville dynasty, the dissolute and predatory Alec d'Urberville, who drugs and rapes her, making her pregnant. Tess's child dies in infancy after it was refused baptism by the parson because it was born in sin.

Some years later, while working on a dairy farm, Tess meets and falls in love with Angel Clare, who believes Tess to be virtuous and pure: a child of nature. Angel and Tess marry but on their wedding night Tess confesses about her past trauma and Angel, feeling his idealized image of her is tarnished beyond repair, abandons her. Further misfortune befalls Tess and her family before she is forced to enter into an abusive arrangement with Alec, her former tormentor, in order to secure the financial survival of her family.

Hardy portrays Tess as an innocent victim who suffers great and tragic injustice. He is withering in his criticism of the hypocritical double standards of Victorian morality. The men in Tess's life dominate and abuse her in different ways. Her father seeks to exploit her financially through her labour, Alec seeks to own her purely for his lustful gratifications, and the pious Angel puts her on a pedestal as a paragon of purity and virtue but then abandons her when his exacting standards are not met (while hypocritically excusing his own previous sexual relationships). *Tess of the d'Urbervilles* presents 'the fallen woman' narrative but portrays Tess not as a victim of circumstance or fatal flaws, but as a victim of the condemnatory and exploitative attitude to women in Victorian society.

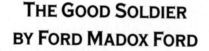

THE GOOD SOLDIER
BY FORD MADOX FORD

SYNOPSIS

The tragic story of Edward Ashburnham and his seemingly perfect marriage which unravels through adultery, and his relationship with another couple.

LIFE LESSON

Adultery is a disruptive force which morally corrupts. Appearances can be deceptive, as things are not always as they seem.

Recounting the story of two wealthy, upper-middle-class couples, *The Good Soldier* (1915) tells how their supposedly perfect marriages are destroyed through countless betrayals and deceptions. The novel is narrated by one member of the foursome, John Dowell, in a series of flashbacks which are not presented chronologically and give only his impressions of the inter-relationships, intrigues and tangled web of deceit.

As more and more information is divulged by Dowell, inconsistencies in his account start to become apparent, and his claims to be merely an impartial, dispassionate bystander to all the emotional chaos are called into question. Is Dowell's account reliable, or is he glossing over things or possibly hiding his own part in the manipulations that occur? Could

Dowell have committed murders which he has covered up as suicides?

The Good Soldier is an underrated thriller/melodrama which makes subtle use of the literary device of the unreliable narrator. There is a certain pleasure to be had from trying to trace through Dowell's flashbacks to ascertain what is real and what is artifice, and this disparity between appearance and reality is one of the key themes of the novel. For example, Dowell regularly refers to characters in the novel as 'good people' even though, by any measure of moral behaviour, most of them certainly are not.

THE GOD OF SMALL THINGS
BY ARUNDHATI ROY

SYNOPSIS

A family drama focusing on the lives of
twins growing up in a wealthy family in the
Kerala region of India in the late 1960s,
and examining the discrimination and
prejudice of the Indian caste system.

LIFE LESSON

Love is such a powerful force driving human
behaviour that it cannot be constrained by societal
codes that seek to restrict who can be loved by whom.

The God of Small Things centres on the Ipe family, Syrian Christians who are relatively wealthy business owners in the Kerala region of India. At the core of the story are fraternal twins Rahel, a girl, and Estha, a boy. The action starts in 1969 when the twins are seven years old, but moves backwards and forwards to 1993. The twins befriend the kindly Velutha, a worker in the family's pickle factory, who becomes a sort of surrogate father. Velutha, however, is a *Dalit* or untouchable, a member of the lowest caste, and when he begins a clandestine and forbidden affair with Ammu, the twin's mother, it sets off a chain of events leading to a life-changing tragedy.

The God of Small Things examines forbidden love through three generations of the Ipe family. The maternal great aunt, Baby Kochamma, is driven to bitterness and spite by her unrequited love for a Catholic priest. The love affair between Velutha and Ammu transgresses caste lines and ultimately destroys the family. At the end of the novel, having been separated for many years, the reunited twins bond by having incestuous sex, the ultimate forbidden love.

Roy seems to suggest that rigid societal constraints on the power of love only lead to negative consequences, sadness and loss. Her first novel, *The God of Small Things* sharply divides opinion. It was heavily criticized and initially banned in parts of India on the grounds of its graphic depiction of sexuality. It was a controversial winner of the Booker Prize in 1997, the year of its publication.

A ROOM WITH A VIEW
BY E.M. FORSTER

SYNOPSIS

A pretty, upper-class English woman is touring Italy when she becomes involved in a romance with an unconventional young man from an upwardly mobile background.

LIFE LESSON

Passion, spontaneity and following your heart's desires are more important foundations for a relationship than stability and social class conventions.

At its heart *A Room with a View* (1908) is a love story, detailing the dilemma of a sheltered young debutante, Lucy Honeychurch, who is torn between the affections and attentions of two very different men. On one hand, there is the impulsive, romantic, rough diamond George Emerson, a product of the new middle class, and on the other hand there is Cecil Vyse, the foppish, pretentious upper-class aesthete. The action switches from the beautiful backdrop of Florence and its surrounding hills to the rural Surrey countryside, with the theme of nature very much a counterpoint to the turmoil in Lucy's heart.

This novel is also, however, an acutely observed critique of the social values and manners of Edwardian England in the early twentieth century. In particular, it shows the conflict between the old ways of snobbish propriety, as embodied by Lucy's chaperone cousin Charlotte Bartlett, and the freethinking, modern attitudes of Mr Emerson. The book reads at times as an almost pitch-perfect parody of a Jane Austen novel, particularly with Forster's sharp ear for ironic witticisms: 'It is so difficult – at least, I find it difficult – to understand people who speak the truth,' says Mr Beebe, an Anglican clergyman whose vocation is surely founded on speaking the truth.

Time and again Forster litters his novel with these wonderful paradoxes: 'You will never repent of a little civility to your inferiors. *That is the true democracy,*' declares the novelist Eleanor Lavish, inadvertently undermining her pretence at being a democrat.

The satire is subtle and gentle, however, and so masterfully executed that with the exception possibly of the insufferable Cecil (although he, too, has his moments), it is hard not to view the characters, for all their snobbery and elitism, as a harmless group of eccentric relics from a bygone age.

THE LADY WITH THE DOG
BY ANTON CHEKHOV

SYNOPSIS

Celebrated, cerebral story detailing an extramarital affair between a cynical Moscow financier and a younger married woman.

LIFE LESSON

The power of love can enter the lives
of even the most world-weary people
and radically transform them.

Published in 1899, this is a short story by an acknowledged master of the form. A cynical and bored Moscow banker, Dimitri Gurov, starts an affair with Anna Sergeyevna, a younger married woman, while on holiday in Yalta. Dimitri is approaching middle age and has long tired of his life, particularly his loveless marriage to a wife he is serially unfaithful to. His interest in Anna is initially superficial and merely something to pass the time and amuse himself. When Anna is suddenly called back home, Dimitri goes with her to the train station to say goodbye, believing that to be the end of their affair.

However, after returning to Moscow and slipping back into the routine of his old life, Dimitri becomes increasingly restless and distracted. He is haunted by his memories of Anna, and surprised by the feelings that she has stirred in him. Desperate to see her again, he travels to St Petersburg to find her and they begin a long-distance secret affair.

Chekhov beautifully describes the complex emotional turmoil of his principal characters, particularly the journey of self-realization that Dimitri embarks upon through his affair with Anna. In the final scene, they meet in a Moscow hotel and discuss their relationship, the pain of separation, and the deceit and secrecy shrouding their affair. The story ends with this moment of unresolved ambiguity:

'… *it was clear to both of them that they had still a long, long road before them, and that the most complicated and difficult part of it was only just beginning.*'

The Lady with the Dog is Chekhov at the height of his powers. The story shows a fleeting snapshot of two lives that entwine and the raw emotions of the protagonists, drawn with a melancholy tone and dry lack of sentimentality or judgement.

CHAPTER 2

PEOPLE AND SOCIETY

It is often said that truly great literature acts as a mirror to society, reflecting its attitudes and manners, philosophies, politics and people at a particular time. This idea is referred to by sociologists as 'reflection theory', and is based on the notion that the social and cultural context of a work of literature has a direct influence on its narrative perspective. Reflection theory, although a useful starting point for analysing the sociological impact of literature, assumes that works of realist fiction transparently document the social world they seek to describe, dispassionately and without bias or prejudice. Literature, however, is a construct of language, and in seeking to describe the world it does so selectively, amplifying some objects of the social world it seeks to elucidate often at the expense of others it reduces or neglects.

The novels discussed in this chapter are often critical of the societies they seek to describe – the social and class structures, manners and attitudes. Social realism in fiction flourished in the nineteenth century with British writers such as Charles Dickens, George Eliot and William Makepeace Thackeray depicting the trials and tribulations of everyday lives to illuminate issues of social injustice, the plight of the poor and the tyranny of institutions. However, realism is not the only method for providing a critique of society. Works of satire, absurdist literature and science fiction can equally provide withering assessments of society's ills and the people who populate it.

DAVID COPPERFIELD
BY CHARLES DICKENS

SYNOPSIS

The memoirs of a man who suffers great hardships and challenges throughout a life which is coloured by his encounters with many extraordinary and eccentric characters.

LIFE LESSON

Money troubles cause much misery and hardship so it is advisable, where possible, to try to live within our means.

When the eponymous hero of this novel is sent to work in London, he finds lodging with the Micawber family. The head of the house, Wilkins Micawber, is a skilled orator, prone to florid pronouncements and a repeated hopeful assertion (usually in the face of financial ruin) that 'something will turn up'. The young David is the recipient of Micawber's wisdom and advice, most notably on the subject of fiscal prudence:

> *"My other piece of advice, Copperfield," said Mr. Micawber, "you know. Annual income twenty pounds, annual expenditure nineteen nineteen and six, result happiness. Annual income twenty pounds, annual expenditure twenty pounds ought and six, result misery."*

The irony, of course, is that Micawber is completely incapable of following his own advice and is pursued throughout the novel by his creditors, spending time in a debtors' prison. However, despite his chronic inability to manage his affairs, Micawber is redeemed by the role he plays in exposing the cheating Uriah Heep, and is rewarded with a new and prosperous life when he and his family emigrate to Australia.

Published in 1850, *David Copperfield* is the most semi-autobiographical of Dickens' novels. His own father was imprisoned for debt, and he had first-hand experience of financial hardship in his childhood.

DEAD SOULS BY NIKOLAI GOGOL

SYNOPSIS

The adventures of Pavel Ivanovich Chichikov, a travelling confidence trickster who executes a bizarre plan to purchase the 'dead souls' of serfs from gullible and greedy provincial Russian aristocrats.

LIFE LESSON

Self-centred ambition and greed often entail corruption, and if something seems too good to be true, that is because it usually is.

Gogol's darkly comic masterpiece opens with Chichikov arriving in a small rural city referred to throughout the novel as N. Chichikov sets about ingratiating himself with local dignitaries and aristocrats by charming and flattering them. He offers to save them money by purchasing ownership of dead serfs.

Imperial Russia at the time *Dead Souls* was written (1842) was organized along feudal lines. Landowners owned serfs, lowly peasants who worked for them and farmed their estates in return for accommodation and bare subsistence. Serfs were regarded as taxable commodities and were counted in national censuses, which were undertaken sporadically and were riddled with bureaucratic inaccuracies. Serfs had a very short life expectancy on account of the atrocious living conditions many were forced to endure, so landowners often found themselves paying tax on deceased serfs for many years between censuses.

Chichikov's plan, therefore, was to buy ownership rights of dead serfs (serfs were counted for official purposes as 'souls') and then fraudulently borrow vast sums of money against the value the serfs would have been worth had they been alive.

Dead Souls is traditionally considered as a reformist satire on the institution of serfdom. As barbaric as the Russian feudal system seems to modern readers (it was another two decades before serfdom was abolished in 1861), Gogol's real target was the fickleness and stupidity of the Russian provincial aristocracy. The people Chichikov encounters are paranoid, neurotic, pretentious and amoral, and are the real 'dead souls' of the novel. There is a specific Russian word, *poshlost*, which Gogol invokes to describe a particular type of privileged philistinism prevalent in the landowning aristocracy of the time.

Did You Know?

Gogol originally intended *Dead Souls* to be in three parts, loosely aligned to the scheme of Dante's *Divine Comedy*. The first, completed, part corresponds to Dante's inferno, with the planned second and third parts representing purgatory and paradise. Gogol struggled with writing the second part, largely due to failing health but also because he felt that he had portrayed the 'hellish' characters in part one to such great effect it might diminish the power of the satire if he started writing nice things about the Russian people.

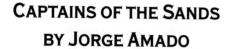

CAPTAINS OF THE SANDS
BY JORGE AMADO

SYNOPSIS

The tale of a gang of children living on the streets of Salvador, Brazil. The children live by their wits and survive by begging, gambling and petty crime, but are ostracized by society and discriminated against by the police and the authorities.

LIFE LESSON

There is no price that can be placed on the value of love, security and compassion.

This is one of the most popular works of twentieth-century Brazilian fiction. Published in 1937, it recounts the harsh realities of life on the streets for a group of abandoned, outcast children, the 'captains' of the title. Living from hand to mouth, the children beg and steal in order to survive yet are bound together by loyalty to each other. One of the characters, known only as Legless, uses his deformed leg to trick his way into the homes of the wealthy to scout for future burglaries. However, one of his potential victims, Dona Ester, is mourning the tragic death of her own child, so takes Legless into her home, treating him with love and compassion. This causes agonising conflict for Legless, as he is overwhelmed by the woman's unconditional kindness and the promise of a life of love and security that he craves, but is torn by his loyalty to the captains:

'She went out, closing the door. Legless stood stock still, not moving, not even answering her "good night," his hand to his face at the spot where Dona Ester had kissed him. He wasn't thinking, wasn't seeking anything. Only the soft caress of the kiss, a caress such as he had never had, a mother's caress. Only the soft caress on his face. It was as if the world had stopped at the moment of the kiss and everything had changed. In the whole universe there was only the soft feel of that maternal kiss on Legless's face.'

The Burning of a Literary Classic

A vocal member of the Brazilian Communist Party, Amado's leftist views were at odds with the populist regime of President Getúlio Vargas. On publication, nearly a thousand copies of *Captains of the Sands* were publicly burned along with works by other writers that the authorities deemed subversive or communist propaganda. The novel survived initial suppression and is considered a cult classic and an important work of socialist realism.

I AM A CAT
BY NATSUME SŌSEKI

SYNOPSIS

Satirical novel concerning the humdrum
lives of a middle-class Japanese family along
with their friends and neighbours, as seen
through the eyes of a domestic cat.

LIFE LESSON

Self-knowledge is key to understanding life,
and can be attained by careful observation of
our own and others' manners and behaviour.

A beloved work, *I Am a Cat* was published in 1906 but is still
a regular feature of the Japanese school curriculum. The plot,
in as much as one exists, concerns a domestic cat who wanders
around his neighbourhood eavesdropping on his owners and
their friends, and making cynical and sardonic observations
on human faults and frailties. The episodic structure of the
novel is largely due to the fact that the book was originally
serialized in a literary magazine. The cat narrator 'speaks' in
a florid and highfaluting authorial voice which emphasizes
his sense of superiority and is a running joke throughout
the story. Early in the novel, the cat surmises that humans
are largely selfish and self-serving, but later on laments that

humans would be far happier if they were more aware of their flaws and weaknesses:

> *'The important thing in life, whether we speak of animals or humankind, is knowing the self. If humans would only learn to know themselves, they'd deserve more respect than any cat. I might even feel uncomfortable about treating them as caricatures in that case and put aside this poison pen of mine. Alas, ... it appears they know as little about themselves as they do about the sizes of their own noses.'*

A HANDFUL OF DUST
BY EVELYN WAUGH

SYNOPSIS

A satirical novel detailing the disintegration of a marriage between two wealthy but shallow socialites, and the aftermath of their divorce.

LIFE LESSON

An obsession with money and status can lead to amorality and spiritual bankruptcy.

Many critics consider this novel, published in 1934, to be among Evelyn Waugh's finest works. It is populated by characters so bereft of any redeeming features it is hard to have any sympathy for any of them. Tony Last, the protagonist, is a country squire of no notable talent but considerable wealth. Brenda, his wife, is a bored socialite who is conducting an affair purely to give herself something to do. This cynical disregard for other people permeates the book, as the various characters pursue their own self-interests which usually revolve around money and social status.

Eventually, Tony tries to change his life by embarking on an expedition to the Amazon jungle in search of a mythical city. Becoming lost in the rainforest, he is taken captive by a Mr Todd, a deeply disturbed man who forces Tony to spend his days reading out loud to him the works of Charles Dickens. The savagery of the jungle neatly mirrors the social savagery of upper-middle-class England.

DIARY OF A MADMAN
BY LU XUN

SYNOPSIS
The delusions of a man who develops a persecution complex believing that the inhabitants of his village are plotting to do him harm and are members of a cult practising cannibalism.

LIFE LESSON

Satirical attack on traditional Chinese culture
of the early twentieth century and, in a wider
sense, societies where the strong metaphorically
devour the weak and downtrodden.

Comprising thirteen fragments from a diary detailing the paranoia of a man who feels outcast from society, this novella was published in 1918. Lu Xun took an 1835 short story of the same title by Russian satirist Nikolai Gogol as his model, using mental illness as a metaphor for the suppression of the individual in corrupt and authoritarian societies. The madman is never referred to by name, and, as his sense of being persecuted by those around him – including his family – increases, so does his disgust for the norms of society.

Believing his fellow villagers to be cannibals, at one point, when interacting with a young man, the madman questions the ethics of eating people and asks, 'But is it right?' Tellingly, the young man replies that he doesn't understand the question. This is a metaphor for how little dissent there was against corrupt and dehumanizing elements in traditional imperial Chinese society: either conform or be consumed.

Diary of a Madman is often considered to be a watershed moment in Chinese culture. Lu Xun was well versed in European and particularly Russian writings, and used techniques of symbolism and metaphor in his satirical social critiques to form a new type of Chinese literature.

Did You Know?

Diary of a Madman was one of the first works of literature to be written in vernacular Chinese. Written Chinese was historically based upon a classical form of the language passed down through imperial dynasties. By 1918, a progressive group of scholars argued that the classical form was elitist and far removed from how people communicated in everyday life. They promoted a new written standard known as *baihua*. This incorporated local dialects and figures of speech, foreign loan words and a punctuation system (Classical Chinese is unpunctuated) in a simplified form of Chinese. *Baihua* could be easily taught in schools, thereby boosting literacy and educational equality. Lu Xun's popular writings helped establish this new system.

A Hero of Our Time
by Mikhail Lermontov

Synopsis

The adventures of Grigory Pechorin, a nihilistic
Russian army officer, as he travels through
the Caucasus in the nineteenth century.

Life Lesson

The human ego can have destructive powers, and
modern society can be a spiritual wasteland.

Published in 1840, this is an early example of a particularly
Russian literary trope: the 'superfluous man', a character who is
usually talented or wealthy, but is self-centred and lacks a sense
of purpose. The concept is derived from the Byronic hero, or
in this case, anti-hero. Pechorin is a clever, charismatic army
officer who gets involved in various intrigues and conflicts to
distract himself from his all-pervading sense of boredom and
existential angst. A self-proclaimed nihilist, he is a complex
character. Often diffident, cynical and aloof, he nonetheless has
moments of sensitivity and self-loathing, at one point stating:
'My whole life has been merely a succession of miserable and
unsuccessful denials of feelings or reason.'

The wild landscape of the Russian Caucasus correlates to
the behaviour and personality of Pechorin, whose actions

are arbitrary and unpredictable, and to the desolate nature of his soul.

The title of the novel is, of course, ironic. Pechorin is not at all a traditional hero. Lermontov, dismayed by criticism of his novel, revised it, adding a rather terse preface in which he harangued his critics and explained the book's title: 'Pechorin, gentlemen, is in fact a portrait, but not of one man only: he is a composite portrait, made up of all the vices which flourish, full-grown, among the present generation.' Thus, the novel was originally intended to satirize a particular type of spiritually absent, morally bereft individual lost in the futility of their own existence.

A Hero of Our Time is considered one of the masterworks of the golden age of nineteenth-century Russian literature and became the model for later superfluous man novels by Fyodor Dostoevsky, Ivan Turgenev and Ivan Goncharov (see *Oblomov*). It can also be seen as a precursor to the existential novels of the twentieth century.

1984
BY GEORGE ORWELL

SYNOPSIS

A science-fiction novel and work of political and social satire. It describes the sinister workings of a totalitarian state in the not-too-distant future and one man's futile attempts at resistance and rebellion.

LIFE LESSON

Language is essential in shaping and forming human thought processes. The control and manipulation of language for political gain leads to the suppression of an individual's rights to freedom of speech, thought, association and action.

This dystopian book is set in a future Great Britain known simply as Airstrip One, a province of Oceania, one of three super-states into which the world is divided. Oceania is a single-party state ruled over by the aptly named 'the Party' under the guidance and all-seeing eye of its supreme leader Big Brother. The novel's protagonist is Winston Smith, whose job at the Ministry of Truth is to rewrite historical records to fit the current statements of the Party's dizzying systems of propaganda. Smith, along with many of Oceania's citizens, lives in a state of heightened fear and paranoia, suspecting his colleagues of either being spies for the Thought Police or members of an underground resistance movement, the Brotherhood. Smith meets and embarks upon a clandestine love affair (free sex is outlawed) with Julia, a co-worker, while harbouring dreams of rebellion and freedom.

Eventually, however, Winston and Julia's affair is exposed and they are imprisoned and tortured to reprogram their minds and make them subservient again to the will of the Party. Ultimately it is Winston's all-pervading sense of fear and weakness that causes his downfall and defeats his yearning for love and freedom.

1984 has proved to be enduringly popular as a cautionary fable on the horrors of totalitarian regimes and their methods of surveillance, thought control and torture to suppress the population and maintain power. Many of the ideas in the book have entered into common use, such as 'thought crime', 'newspeak', 'doublethink' and 'Big Brother'. Orwell wrote *1984* while battling tuberculosis, which may in part account for the bleakness of its vision (he died seven months after the novel was published in 1949). As a description of how totalitarian societies promote fear, division and conflict, *1984* stands alongside other dystopian classics such as Aldous Huxley's *Brave New World* (1932) and Yevgeny Zemyatin's *We* (1924).

Did You Know?

It is often claimed that Orwell came up with the title for the novel by simply inverting the year in which he completed it, 1948. This has led to speculation that rather than being a prophecy of a bleak dystopian future, Orwell was satirizing the world as he saw it, or the direction in which some societies were heading. However, the original working title was *The Last Man in Europe*, which was then changed to *1982* before Orwell finally settled on *1984*. Hence, the inversion theory may be mere coincidence.

A CLOCKWORK ORANGE
BY ANTHONY BURGESS

SYNOPSIS

In a futuristic, dystopian society, a violent teenage gang leader is sent to prison for rape and murder. He volunteers for a neurological reprogramming experiment to 'cure' him of his vicious tendencies.

LIFE LESSON

Free will and the freedom to choose between good and evil underpins human morality. Withdraw that choice, and humans are reduced to automatons.

A Clockwork Orange (1962) is narrated by its protagonist Alex, a fifteen-year-old leader of a street gang, in an invented argot called 'nadsat' (a mix of London slang, anglicized borrowings and cross-lingual puns from other languages, most notably Russian). After indulging in an orgy of violence, Alex is apprehended by the police and convicted of murder. While in prison Alex commits another murder, then takes part in an experimental behavioural modification programme, an extreme form of aversion therapy. On release from prison and seemingly 'cured' of his violent tendencies, Alex struggles to adapt to his new life. His capacity to choose between right and wrong has been stripped away, and without that he is not able to choose a path to redemption or real rehabilitation. He ends up an unwitting pawn in anti-government propaganda, and attempts to commit suicide.

Burgess' novel is a bleak political and social satire that highlights the insidious methods through which governments manipulate crime in order to control individuals and keep society in a state of fear and passive submission.

THE PRIME OF MISS JEAN BRODIE BY MURIEL SPARK

SYNOPSIS

An outspoken and unconventional schoolteacher adopts a radical approach to the education of a group of young girls under her guidance.

LIFE LESSON

In education there is an often blurred distinction between encouraging freethinking and progressive attitudes, and imposing personal opinions and prejudices.

On the surface, this novel seems to follow a familiar narrative trope, established in many books and films, of a progressive and inspirational teacher who becomes a victim of the established orthodoxy and/or is betrayed by petty jealousy.

In an Edinburgh girls' school in the 1930s, Miss Jean Brodie encourages her pupils to embrace the powers of art, literature, religion and romance at the expense of mathematics and science. Often at loggerheads with the headteacher, Brodie encourages her 'set' of six carefully groomed girls to rebel against the conventions of the time.

Beneath the surface, however, the novel is an exploration of much more complex and sinister psychologies. Brodie carefully selects the set she mentors, playing upon their neediness and insecurities. She encourages them to exclude others, manipulates them in thought and deed, and even attempts to embroil one of the students in an illicit affair with another teacher. Brodie admires and romanticizes fascist dictators such as Mussolini and Franco, and it is this preaching of her warped view of the world which finally leads to her dismissal.

It could be argued that, although set in the 1930s against the backdrop of the rise of fascist ideologies, Spark's book was published in 1961, and is a sly satire on ideas of sexual liberation and freethinking among the post-war generation. The message is that beneath the veneer of supposed freedom and progressive values lies the same fanaticism, exclusion and oppression, just in a different form. A slight novel, written in Spark's beautifully economical prose, *The Prime of Miss Jean Brodie* has many dark subtexts smouldering beneath its seemingly light and airy exterior.

MIDDLEMARCH BY GEORGE ELIOT

SYNOPSIS

Classic Victorian novel depicting the lives of the inhabitants of a provincial town in the Midlands of England. A wide range of characters intersect around themes such as the position of women in society, idealism, ambition and the nature of marriage.

LIFE LESSON

The actions, ambitions and desires of individuals impact upon the people they are surrounded by, and vice versa. Society pressures individuals to conform, yet conformity can stifle personal development.

Often cited as one of the greatest novels of the nineteenth century, *Middlemarch* (1872) bears a resemblance to more modern novels in terms of its imaginative and narrative scope. The subtitle '*A Study of Provincial Life*' is particularly apposite, as Eliot describes in exacting detail the ambitions, interactions, vocations, manners and relationships of an array of different characters. A central theme is the stifling institution of marriage, as characters in Middlemarch believe they are marrying for love, but in reality are conforming and compromising to a societal norm.

It was a common trope in Victorian fiction, particularly romantic fiction, to end novels with a wedding, as if this was the highest ideal to which one should aspire in the pursuit of personal happiness and fulfilment. Eliot, whose real name was Mary Anne Evans, had an unconventional relationship with the philosopher and critic George Henry Lewes which was condemned by her family. She subverts the norms of Victorian romantic fiction by portraying marriages as either failures, transactional compromises or vacuous idealism.

Middlemarch is not an easy read. It takes considerable patience to wade through the kaleidoscopic details spread across more than eight hundred and fifty pages, yet it rewards the diligent reader with insight into English society at a time of upheaval and change.

THE ADVENTURES OF HUCKLEBERRY FINN BY MARK TWAIN

SYNOPSIS

The story of a poor white boy who runs away from his alcoholic and abusive father and teams up with an escaped slave. Together, the two embark on an odyssey down the Mississippi River in search of freedom.

LIFE LESSON

Personal freedom and independence can
be found within the natural world. This
contrasts with the artificial values of society
that are found in the cultural world.

This 1884 book is cited as one of the Great American Novels. Although conceived as a sequel to *The Adventures of Tom Sawyer* (1876), *Huckleberry Finn*, as it is usually known, differs radically from its predecessor. Twain deploys the use of a first-person narrator who describes his thoughts and actions in a Southern vernacular with elements of different dialects, figures of speech and broken syntax.

The novel itself is a rite of passage story, with the journey down the Mississippi River mirroring Huck Finn's journey from boyhood to adulthood. In the Homeric tradition of the *Odyssey*, Huck encounters various characters and situations that often present difficult moral decisions and dilemmas, and it requires his wits and intelligence to navigate a safe passage and continue his voyage of self-discovery.

The book attracted controversy on publication and continues to divide critics to this day. One common issue, particularly for modern readers, is the frequent use of the word 'nigger' and other racial slurs and stereotypes. The counter-argument is that the novel is withering in its criticism of slavery and is pointedly anti-racist. The theme of personal freedom is central to the narrative and Twain is scornful of the entrenched attitudes of the 'Old South', as well as its materialism and moral corruption that constrain individuals. Huck and Jim's life on the river is shown to be one of natural freedom, an escape from the stifling 'sivilising' (sic) pressures of society.

Huckleberry Finn is an important book in the history of American literature. With its revolutionary use of regional vernacular, universal themes and critiques of social attitudes, it single-handedly changed the nature of books for children.

Did You Know?

When *Huckleberry Finn* was published in the USA in 1885 (it appeared first in the UK and Canada) it was banned in several places; one libraries board stated that it was 'trash' and 'only suitable for the slums'. Ironically, the initial objections to the novel did not centre on the race issue, but highlighted Twain's use of Southern vernacular, criticizing the writer for 'backwards talking' and using bad language. The contention was that Twain was ridiculing people from the South and, in particular, the way they spoke.

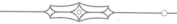

THE GREAT GATSBY
BY F. SCOTT FITZGERALD

SYNOPSIS

Classic novel depicting the hedonism and moral abandon of 1920s New York and telling the tragic tale of Jay Gatsby, a mysterious millionaire, and his pursuit of his lost love.

LIFE LESSON

There is often a disparity between appearances and reality; things are not always what they seem. Money cannot buy happiness or love.

The Great Gatsby was written and published in 1925 during the Roaring Twenties, a time of great economic and social change that was also the beginning of the Jazz Age. The novel is narrated by Nick Carraway, a veteran of the First World War, who has moved to the east coast to try to make his mark in the financial world. Through Carraway's eyes the reader observes the other characters and their relationships, motivations and conceits. Opulence is everywhere in the novel, with descriptions of lavish houses and clothes, and Gatsby's decadent parties. A clear distinction, however, is made between the two localities of East Egg and West Egg. The former is where the inherited 'old' wealth of Tom and

Daisy Buchanan reside, whereas the latter represents the new money of Gatsby and the aspiring Carraway.

The novel is often described as a critique of the American Dream, the idea that the USA is a country of aspiration and reinvention where anybody can become somebody. Gatsby is fabulously wealthy, and Fitzgerald has fun recounting the whispers and rumours as to where his money has come from, but ultimately his prosperity cannot buy him the one thing he craves, his lost love. This is where the American Dream fails, for despite his riches, Gatsby will always be 'Mr Nobody from Nowhere' (as Tom Buchanan dismissively states).

The Great Gatsby is a short novel but manages to cram some big themes into its one hundred and eighty pages. These include moral and social decadence, social stratification, gender roles and the corrupting influence of money. The tale of Jay Gatsby's rise and fall remains as compelling and as relevant today as it did to readers a hundred years ago.

OF MICE AND MEN
BY JOHN STEINBECK

SYNOPSIS

The tragic tale of two migrant ranch workers who dream of owning their own farm during the Great Depression in 1930s America.

LIFE LESSON

Friendship can be a powerful motivation behind
human behaviour. It is dangerous to believe in
dreams as a way of finding meaning in the world.

Barely longer than a novella, this short book is the story of
two itinerate ranch hands, George and Lennie, who travel
from place to place to find work during the Great Depression.
The two men have an enduring dream of one day owning their
own farm.

Throughout the novel, which was published in 1937,
Steinbeck explores the nature of human loneliness and
isolation. Many of the characters verbally express their desire
for friendship. George and Lennie have a bond built upon
George's sense of responsibility, and their shared dream is
to have self-determination and be 'their own boss'. It is an
intoxicating dream, and one which fellow ranch hands Candy,
who desires security and companionship in his old age, and
Crooks, who strives for recognition and self-respect, are
readily seduced by.

The tragedy that unfolds in *Of Mice and Men* is one of
unattainable aspirations that are thwarted by circumstance,
and of people unable to escape the situations they are trapped
in. George has pledged to look after Lennie, who has a mental
disability, but this restricts George's own freedom and has become
a burden that threatens his ambitions. Curley's wife is ensnared
in an unhappy and abusive marriage to the ranch owner's cruel
son and is forced to abandon her dreams of being a famous
movie star. Candy, partially crippled after an accident, is lonely
after the death of his faithful dog and left contemplating old age

alone when he is deemed no longer of use on the ranch. Lennie, through no fault of his own, is imprisoned by his disability and a disorder that compels him to fetishize and touch soft things, making him a danger to himself and others.

In this book's few pages, Steinbeck fashioned a brutal tale of human loneliness and oppression, cruelty and shattered dreams.

Vanity Fair
by William Makepeace Thackeray

Synopsis

The parallel lives of two young women as they strive to make their mark in upper-class English society against the backdrop of the Napoleonic wars.

Life Lesson

Striving for wealth and social status through amoral ways and blind ambition will ultimately end in unhappiness, failure and social isolation.

First serialized in twenty instalments in the satirical magazine *Punch*, *Vanity Fair* was collected into a single volume in 1848. The original parts contained the subtitle *Pen and Pencil Sketches of English Society*, and this perfectly illustrates the style and sardonic tone of the novel. The sprawling plot concerns two young women, Becky Sharp, an orphan, and Amelia 'Emmy' Sedley, a girl from a respectable family. The two are friends, but complete opposites: Becky is ambitious, manipulative and deceitful: she knows what she wants and will stop at nothing to achieve her aims. Amelia is passive, sensitive, virtuous and kind, if a little too innocent of the harsh realities of the world.

The reader follows the girls through various intrigues and marriages, affairs and scandals as they encounter the 'sketches' of the people who populate the upper echelons of early nineteenth-century English society. When the novel was published in a single volume, Thackeray changed the subtitle to *A Novel Without a Hero*, as almost all of the characters display flaws and faults through their vanity, selfishness and greed.

Vanity Fair is considered a classic work of social satire that takes aim at the moral and ethical issues of its time. Marxist critics have argued that one of its main themes is the commodification of women in marriage and that it satirizes the superficial world of early capitalism. Conversely, satire can also be conservative in perspective, striving to preserve the social and cultural customs of the past. Although Thackeray's withering eye ridicules rampant materialism, vanity, snobbery and hypocrisy, he offers no prospect of redemption or reform for society's ills. Perhaps Thackery is really attacking the idea of upwards social mobility itself, believing it erodes old-fashioned values of honesty and decency, as well as reinforcing the idea of 'knowing your place'. The book certainly points out that wealth, however ruthlessly acquired, cannot buy moral qualities.

THE MAGIC MOUNTAIN
BY THOMAS MANN

SYNOPSIS

Philosophical German novel concerning the nature
of illness and disease. It is centred on a young
man confined in an exclusive sanatorium in the
Swiss Alps in the years leading up to the First
World War, and the people he encounters there.

LIFE LESSON

Life is a quest for authentic wisdom and knowledge
that can be grasped through contemplation
and experience of illness and death.

It took twelve years of writing and revising before Thomas
Mann was ready to publish this novel in 1924. It centres on
Hans Castorp, a relatively wealthy young German who is
about to embark on a career as an engineer. Prior to taking up
his new job, Castorp goes to visit his cousin, who is trying to
recover from tuberculosis in a fashionable sanatorium in Davos,
Switzerland. Castorp only intended to stay at the sanatorium
for three weeks to keep his cousin company, but while there
develops a mild bronchial infection. As Castorp's condition
starts to deteriorate he is diagnosed with early symptoms of
tuberculosis, and has to stay there until his health improves.

Castorp is quickly beguiled by life in the sanatorium, especially
its otherworldly setting of staggering alpine beauty and 'eternal

snow'. Life there is one of idleness and leisure, punctuated by often eccentric treatments and medical interventions. Castorp befriends other patients, a wealthy cross-section of the European bourgeoisie, who, despite differences in age, temperament, nationality and language, bond together through their collective experiences of illness and threat of impending death.

The Magic Mountain is a form of *Bildungsroman*, a novel in which a central protagonist undertakes a journey leading to moral, spiritual and intellectual enlightenment. The novel also subverts some elements of the form, in that all of the action occurs in one place. Although Castorp develops a thirst for knowledge and learns from his interactions with the other patients, ultimately it is through his contemplation of death that he gains a greater understanding of life.

Did You Know?

Thomas Mann started writing *The Magic Mountain* in 1912 after visiting his wife who was recuperating from a lung infection at a famous sanatorium in Davos. He began it as a comic short story, but the First World War had a profound effect upon Mann's view of the world. He revisited and expanded the novel to reflect a much darker tone. The disease can be read as an allegory for the deterioration of European society as it descended into the horrors of war.

GARGANTUA AND PANTAGRUEL
BY FRANÇOIS RABELAIS

SYNOPSIS

A series of five sixteenth-century grotesque
and satirical French novels detailing
the lives and adventures of the giants
Pantagruel and his father Gargantua.

LIFE LESSON

There is wisdom and joy in humour
and the ability to not take the world, its
people and society too seriously.

The original French titles of this series are wilfully long and obtuse, so in English it is commonly referred to simply as *Gargantua and Pantagruel*. The first book, *Pantagruel*, published around 1532, details the origin of giants and the birth, early life and education of Pantagruel. The second book, *Gargantua*, acts as a prequel to the first (most modern compendium editions are rearranged with *Gargantua* placed first) and fills in details about Pantagruel's father Gargantua. The remaining three books are an extended parody of the heroic quest of popular medieval romances (see also *Don Quixote*), with the principal aim of the quest to determine if there is any point in Pantagruel's friend Panurge getting married.

Gargantua and Pantagruel is a ribald, scatological satire which lampoons marriage, education, religion, war and just about any aspect of French Renaissance life its author wanted to poke fun at. The novels are brimming with subversions of form, particularly the mock quest where, rather than a virtuous mission to rescue a maiden, Pantagruel and Panurge's aim seems to be to find every possible reason not to save a maiden for fear of being cuckolded. Rabelais was also in love with wordplay and puns, inventing words and making absurd 'wise' proclamations.

Gargantua and Pantagruel typifies two literary genres: 'carnivalesque' and 'grotesque realism'. Carnival or carnivalesque is a literary style that wilfully subverts and inverts traditional forms, drawing its inspiration from the joyous, anarchic abandon of medieval festivals and folk rituals (and of some carnivals and festivals today). Traditional hierarchies and social strictures are overthrown, and common dualities are turned upside down, so that the stupid become the clever, the sacred becomes profane, and so forth. Grotesque realism is the lowering of noble or high ideals and forms to the basest possible level; for Rabelais this usually involved bodily functions and the ludicrous physicality of human anatomy.

Rabelais was one of the earliest European satirists, whose influence is clear in later novels such as *Don Quixote*, *Tristram Shandy* and *Gulliver's Travels*.

METAMORPHOSIS BY FRANZ KAFKA

SYNOPSIS

Gregor Samsa, a much put-upon travelling
salesman, wakes up one morning to find he
has been transformed into a giant insect.
He struggles to deal with his new condition
and the horror and disgust of his family.

LIFE LESSON

Individuals can become alienated from society.
Their identity and sense of self becomes distorted
through exploitation and crushing obligations.

Kafka's 1915 novella is the tragic tale of a man who inexplicably
turns into a giant cockroach. Gregor, the protagonist, struggles
at first to come to terms with his predicament and attempts
to continue as normal, believing the transformation to be
temporary. His family display a range of emotional responses
to Gregor's change, from hostility and revulsion to pity and
sympathy, but ultimately shame and neglect.

Gregor, we learn, was the principal money-earner in the
household, and part of his family's initial concern is not for his
health and well-being, but about who is going to pay the rent
if Gregor does not work. Gregor is treated with similar callous
indifference and exploitation in his place of work, and yet his
main concern when discovering he had turned into a giant

insect was how it might affect his job. It is striking that his sister Grete is the only one of Gregor's family to question why he has turned into an insect or how he might be feeling. When she eventually turns away from him it is one of the most truly heartbreaking moments in literature.

Metamorphosis is often cited as either absurdist or existential, but it can also be read as an allegory of the way that long-term terminal illness is stigmatized. Gregor becomes increasingly desolate as his family struggle with his needs, locking him away from the world to ultimately waste away and die from starvation through indifference and neglect. It is a powerful and haunting parable of what it feels like to be human in an inhuman world.

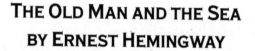

THE OLD MAN AND THE SEA
BY ERNEST HEMINGWAY

SYNOPSIS

An aging Cuban fisherman sets out to snare the catch of his life and becomes involved in an epic battle with a giant marlin.

LIFE LESSON

Perseverance, hope and dignity in the face of defeat are powerful attributes to draw strength from in the course of the struggles and problems of life.

A short novel that came out in 1952, this was Ernest Hemingway's last notable work of fiction that was published in his lifetime. An elderly Cuban fisherman, Santiago, has hit a run of poor luck and has not caught a fish for eighty-four days. Members of his local fishing community are superstitious, and have branded Santiago a 'salao', a colloquial term meaning he is cursed. The superstition has led Santiago to lose the help of his young protégé Manolin, whose family have forced him to work on another boat in the hope of a change of fortune.

Determined to break the hex, Santiago sets off to fish far out to sea and becomes involved in an epic and exhausting tussle with a giant marlin. The struggle lasts for several days and nights until finally Santiago prevails. The fisherman's troubles are not at an end, however, as he has strayed far from land and, injured and fatigued, he must navigate shark-infested waters to get home.

In *The Old Man and the Sea*, Hemingway elevates a simple tale of a man battling against the forces of nature to an allegory of the human spirit and resilience in the face of life's struggles. Santiago sees his battle with the marlin as a noble one between two equals, and recognizes that the challenges the fish poses bring out the best human qualities of hope, courage, love and persistence. Semi-delirious through lack of sleep, Santiago at some points refers to the marlin as his 'brother', and speculates that it may be a sin to kill the beast. Although Santiago wins the battle, he loses the war as his catch is devoured by sharks. However, his spirit remains unbowed, and he vows to continue to strive, stating at the end: 'Man is not made for defeat. A man can be destroyed but not defeated.'

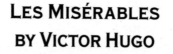

LES MISÉRABLES
BY VICTOR HUGO

SYNOPSIS

Epic French novel of perseverance, courage, love and redemption centring on the trials and tribulations of ex-convict Jean Valjean, who tries to live a life of moral certitude while facing overpowering social injustice and prejudice.

LIFE LESSON

Love, compassion and forgiveness are universal human qualities. To bestow them upon others is a great gift that helps to build a just and free society.

Les Misérables is a mammoth novel, considered to be one of the greatest books of all time, and has inspired countless adaptations on stage and screen, most notably the world's longest running musical show.

Published in 1862, the book follows the peasant Jean Valjean, who, having been released from prison, vows to do good in the world and fight against injustice. Over several decades of his life, we see Valjean try to escape his past, while being relentlessly pursued by the obsessive and vindictive policeman Javert. The story culminates in the Paris Uprising of 1832.

Hugo uses the plot as a canvas to critique pressing social issues of nineteenth-century France including poverty and the distribution of wealth, the treatment of women, industrialization, social justice and republicanism. The novel is also something of an encyclopaedia of French history, containing frequent digressions on a variety of subjects which often have little direct relevance to the actual narrative, but place the novel firmly in its historical context.

Ploughing through this novel of more than 1,400 pages (the original French manuscript contains over 655,000 words) is a labour of love, although hardy readers (if they can stomach the digressions) are rewarded not only with a sense of achievement but also with a timeless tale of forgiveness, mercy and redemption.

Great Expectations by Charles Dickens

Synopsis

A coming-of-age novel following the rise to prominence of Pip, an orphan who wishes to become a gentleman and escape his lowly status.

Life Lesson

Love, loyalty and kindness are important values. They underpin a moral conscience and are the basis for genuine relationships, as opposed to the shallow values of material wealth and social status.

This is one of Dickens' best-loved novels and contains some of his most memorable characters. Essentially a Gothic romance and *Bildungsroman,* the story is narrated by Pip, an apprentice blacksmith who aspires to be a gentleman of wealth and sophistication. The novel opens with one of Dickens' most vivid and striking scenes, when Pip meets Magwitch, an escaped convict, in a churchyard. Pip provides food and drink for the convict and a means to cut off his shackles, a kindness that Magwitch never forgets.

While still a young boy, Pip is employed as a playmate for Estella, the adopted daughter of the enigmatic Miss Havisham. Pip quickly falls in love with Estella, then receives news that he has an anonymous benefactor who has provided considerable sums for him to go to London and be educated in the ways of a gentleman.

Published in 1861, *Great Expectations* explores many common Dickensian themes such as social class, the corrupting power of wealth, and crime and justice. The 'great expectations' that Pip has is that through self-improvement, wealth and social standing he will be elevated as a person of good character, when conversely it is his desire for status that ultimately corrupts his moral judgements.

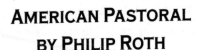

AMERICAN PASTORAL
BY PHILIP ROTH

SYNOPSIS

A successful businessman's 'perfect life'
unravels during the tumultuous political
events of 1960s and early 1970s America.

LIFE LESSON

An individual's expectations of how life should
be can often be very different to the grim
reality of life as it really is. This is especially
true once the thin veneer of respectability
and appearance are stripped away.

This 1997 novel recounts the life of Seymour 'the Swede' Levov,
a businessman who owns a successful glove factory. Roth uses
a framing device of a narrator, Nathan Zuckerman, who was
friends with Seymour's brother Jerry, learning of 'the Swede's'
crumbling world at a high-school reunion. Zuckerman then
tries to reimagine the catastrophic downfall of his friend's
brother against the backdrop of key historical incidents of civil
unrest and political strife.

Seymour epitomizes the American Dream, the son of
Jewish immigrants who have acquired all the trappings of
upper-middle-class respectability. He is a high-school athletics

hero who marries a beauty queen, has a successful business, a beautiful house in the suburbs and a daughter, Merry, over whom he dotes. Merry has a debilitating speech impediment and suffers from anxiety, which alienates her and is the cause of considerable stress and frustration. Various attempts to address the problem of Merry's stutter fail to solve the issue and Merry becomes more disconnected, beginning to attach herself to radical political causes as a means of self-expression. Eventually Merry's radicalization reaches its apotheosis when she plants a bomb in the local post office which kills an innocent bystander – an act which causes Seymour's world to collapse around him.

Roth's novel intertwines and references various historical events from modern US history, including the anti-Vietnam War protests, the Newark Riots of 1967, the activities of left-wing paramilitary groups such as the Weathermen and the Black Panthers, and the Watergate Scandal, to provide context and contrast between Seymour's idyllic pastoral life and the grim reality of much of American society during the period in which the novel is set. *American Pastoral* won the Pulitzer Prize for fiction in 1998, ending a long losing streak for its author, who had been unsuccessfully nominated on three previous occasions.

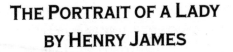

THE PORTRAIT OF A LADY
BY HENRY JAMES

SYNOPSIS

A young and beautiful American heiress travels
to Europe where she is manipulated into a
loveless marriage by two scheming American
expatriates who have designs on her inheritance.

LIFE LESSON

Personal freedom and individuality
can become crushed under the cynical
trappings and expectations of a society
that has superficial materialistic values.

In *The Portrait of a Lady* (1881) Henry James explores a common
theme in his fiction, namely the friction between the values of
the Old World and the New World. The American Isabel Archer
is very much of the New World. She is fiercely independent,
has a thirst for travel and experiences, and does not wish to
be subjugated by the Old World expectation that she should
be nothing more than a dutiful and obliging wife. Throughout
the first part of the novel, Isabel turns down several marriage
proposals, as she is determined to keep her independence.

The turning point comes when Isabel unexpectedly inherits
a considerable fortune. Up to this point she had moderate

social status, but her good fortune immediately pushes her up the social stratum, and she inevitably becomes the object of covetous and corrupting desire. Isabel marries Gilbert Osmond, mistakenly believing that as Osmond is of modest means they will marry as equals. Unbeknown to Isabel, she is the victim of a grand manipulation by Osmond and his mistress Madame Merle to gain access to her fortune. Through Osmond's bullying and coercive control, Isabel's free spirit is ground down as she faces a moral dilemma: to live a life that she most dreads by fulfilling her duties as a wife despite her unhappiness, or escape and recover her freedom and independence?

The Portrait of a Lady shows how New World values of liberty, independence and self-expression clash with the Old World values of social status, duty and, most of all, the thin veneer of appearances. The novel is considered one of Henry James' early masterpieces and the bridge between his early realist novels, and his more experimental and complex later fiction.

THE LORD OF THE FLIES
BY WILLIAM GOLDING

SYNOPSIS

A group of schoolboys are marooned on
a remote island without any adults after
their plane crashes and are forced to fend
for themselves in order to survive.

LIFE LESSON

When isolated from the guidance of
civilization's moral and ethical codes, human
beings revert to savagery and barbarism.

The inspiration for this book, published in 1954, was a nineteenth-century work of young adult fiction, *The Coral Island: A Tale of the Pacific Ocean* (1857) by Scottish writer R.M. Ballantyne. In Ballantyne's 'boys own' adventure, three young survivors of a shipwreck are stranded on a desert island, but learn to live by their wits. They are resourceful and brave, and are portrayed as a civilizing influence on the perceived primitivism of the natives they encounter.

Golding enjoyed the book as a child. He encountered it again when working as an English teacher at a boys' grammar school, and was inspired to write a similar book from an inverse perspective. What if the evil and savagery came from within and was manifest inside the boys themselves? This question is posed by the cerebral and saintly Simon in *Lord of the Flies* halfway through the novel.

In Golding's novel the boys at first forge an uneasy but cooperative alliance, although tensions between two of the 'alpha' boys, Ralph and Jack, gradually rise to the surface and a power struggle develops. Paranoia, superstition and the bloodthirsty and brutal thrill of hunting and killing for food grip the boys in a collective mania leading to violence, cruelty and murder. Golding suggests that humans have an innate capacity for evil and that under certain conditions, namely the absence of clear moral codes provided by religion and laws provided by governments, evil could flourish and become all-encompassing.

Lord of the Flies depicts a brutal view of a society unravelling and descending into darkness and savagery. The novel is set against the backdrop of an unnamed war, and in one sense it can be seen as an allegory for the atrocities of the Second World War which Golding witnessed first-hand as an officer in the Royal Navy.

WISE BLOOD
BY FLANNERY O'CONNOR

SYNOPSIS

A tragicomic parable about religious faith, sin and redemption. A veteran of the Second World War, suffering from post-traumatic stress disorder, returns home to his native Tennessee and, after abandoning his Christian fundamentalist upbringing, sets himself up as a preacher of anti-religion.

LIFE LESSON

It is a terrible irony that the things we most seek to deny and suppress in ourselves are often, paradoxically (and destructively), what we most need and desire.

There can be few more memorable anti-heroes in twentieth-century American fiction than Hazel Motes in this Southern

Gothic masterpiece. Freshly discharged from the army after the Second World War, Hazel embarks upon a quest for truth and spiritual redemption. Feeling abandoned by God, Hazel sets himself up as a street preacher and founds his own missionary movement, 'The Church without Christ'.

Hazel's journey to redemption brings him into contact and conflict with a collection of grotesque and ethically questionable characters, from prostitutes to con artists, as he struggles to come to terms with rejecting his faith but at the same time wondering how he can atone for his sins and spread the word of righteous truth.

Published in 1952, *Wise Blood* is a beautifully written novel, full of dark humour and Gothic horror. It is laced with sardonic asides which question but, perhaps, ultimately affirm, the role of religion in a world so seemingly irreligious in many ways. As O'Connor slyly remarks, 'Faith is what someone knows to be true, whether they believe it or not.'

Did You Know?

A prolific short-story writer, Flannery O'Connor completed only two novels during her tragically short lifetime. She died at the age of thirty-nine from complications from lupus, a terminal auto-immune deficiency disease.

TO KILL A MOCKINGBIRD
BY HARPER LEE

SYNOPSIS

A widowed white lawyer in the Deep South of
the USA takes on a case to defend a black man
unjustly accused of raping a white woman.

LIFE LESSON

An exploration of social morality and the
belief in people as either essentially good or
essentially evil, and an examination of the
impact of prejudice and injustice in society.

Published in 1960, *To Kill a Mockingbird* is one of the most
popular and best-loved novels in the English language, having
sold more than 40 million copies worldwide. It is a coming-
of-age story told by a young girl, nicknamed Scout, who lives
in Alabama with her father and older brother. Scout recounts
incidents from her childhood, the games she and her brother
Jem and best friend Dill play together, and in particular their
fascination with a shadowy and elusive neighbour, Arthur
'Boo' Radley.

Scout's father Atticus Finch agrees to defend a black
man, Tom Robinson, who Atticus believes has been unfairly
accused of the rape of a white woman. Atticus' decision has

wider ramifications for the community, and leads the children into contact with darker elements in society as they experience the effects and tragic consequences of prejudice, intolerance and injustice.

One of the key themes of *To Kill a Mockingbird* is the transition from a state of childhood innocence to one of experience and recognition. Scout and Jem are shunned and taunted at school over their father's defence of Tom Robinson, and struggle to understand the motivations of their tormentors and the attitudes of some of the townsfolk. When Tom Robinson is found guilty by the racially biased jury, Jem is horrified by the injustice of it all and becomes disillusioned with his community. This event signals a rite of passage as Jem leaves childhood behind and becomes a young man who, from experience, has acquired compassion and empathy as well as an understanding that evil and injustice exist in the world.

GULLIVER'S TRAVELS BY JONATHAN SWIFT

SYNOPSIS

Satirical novel detailing a series of sea journeys to a collection of fantastical islands undertaken by a sea captain, and the adventures and people he encounters.

LIFE LESSON

Truth and morality are relative. They exist
in relation to a culture, society, or historical
context, and are fluid not absolute.

The eponymous hero of this book journeys to some of imaginative literature's most memorable places. Gulliver's first voyage takes him (after a shipwreck) to the island of Lilliput, where he finds himself a giant among people who are no bigger than 6 inches (15.2 cm) tall. Subsequent voyages take him to Brobdingnag, the polar opposite of Lilliput, where he is surrounded by giants, and a flying island named Laputa full of crazed scientists, before he eventually travels to the land of the Houyhnhnms, a country inhabited by cultured, talking horses who have enslaved a race of deformed and savage human-like creatures called the Yahoos.

Published in 1726, *Gulliver's Travels* is an example of Menippean satire, a literary genre that satirizes social attitudes and cultural constructs as opposed to specific people or institutions. Menippean satire is typically scattergun in its approach, veering from one target to the next and piling allegory on top of parody. Swift's novel parodies the 'travellers' tales' literary subgenre and also deliberately inverts the supposed realism of contemporary novels of the time such as *Robinson Crusoe*. Swift has tremendous fun at the expense of various targets including royalty, politicians, the Anglo–Irish situation and the Royal Academy of Arts and Science. The novel is also considered one of the first works of science fiction and fantasy.

THE BONFIRE OF THE VANITIES
BY TOM WOLFE

SYNOPSIS

A scornful satire on the greed and hubris of
America in the late 1980s. A wealthy and successful
Wall Street trader in New York is drawn into
a legal and political scandal when his mistress
runs over a black youth. The trader watches
helplessly as his perfect life of privilege unravels.

LIFE LESSON

Money and status do not absolve people of basic
responsibility for the consequences of their actions.

When Sherman McCoy, hotshot WASP bond trader, takes a wrong turn on his way back from the airport it sets off a train of events that snowballs into a full-scale political scandal and media frenzy. During that drive, Sherman and his mistress Maria are confronted by two black youths when they stop to clear some debris blocking a slip road to the highway. Thinking they are about to be robbed, Maria runs over and seriously injures one of the youths. Although Sherman initially suggests they should report the incident to the police, Maria cynically convinces him that the police would not be interested and nobody would care because they were 'in the jungle'.

The arrogance and hubris of the couple triggers their downfall as various characters hijack the ensuing scandal and manipulate and exploit it for their own ends, including a washed-up investigative journalist, corrupt and ambitious lawyers, and local politicians and political activists.

The Bonfire of the Vanities (1987) was originally published in instalments in *Rolling Stone* magazine, as Wolfe had the lofty ambition of emulating his literary heroes Charles Dickens and William Makepeace Thackeray, who first issued most of their novels in serial form. Like them, Wolfe's aim was to 'chronicle' the social, moral (or immoral) and cultural mood of his time, and his novel proved to be a critical and commercial success.

GO TELL IT ON THE MOUNTAIN
BY JAMES BALDWIN

SYNOPSIS

Semi-autobiographical novel about a teenager growing up in Harlem, New York, in the 1930s and his relationships with his family and the local church.

LIFE LESSON

Religion is a source of strength and community, but can also be the cause of repression and moral hypocrisy.

This coming-of-age story about religious faith, sexuality, race and sin centres on John Grimes, a teenager troubled by his relationship with his stepfather and his awakening sexuality. The action takes place on a single day, the protagonist's fourteenth birthday, but deploys flashbacks to flesh out the lives of John's stepfather Gabriel, his mother Elizabeth and his aunt Florence, and their upbringing in the Deep South of the US before they moved north to New York.

Baldwin's novel has religion and the Bible as its central theme. Gabriel is an occasional preacher at the local church and has impressed a strict religious upbringing on his two sons. The novel is littered with religious references and allusions (the title of the novel is a African American spiritual of the same name). The characters' names are also religious, with John correlating to John the Baptist and Gabriel to the archangel.

The second part of the novel is divided into three 'prayers' in the form of flashbacks. These reveal much about the inner thoughts and motivations of the principal characters while reinforcing the role of religion and faith in their lives. At the end of the novel, John has a series of religious hallucinations that cleanse him of his sins and reawaken his commitment to God. *Go Tell It on the Mountain*, published in 1953, explores religious faith in both its positive and negative aspects.

A SMALL, GOOD THING
BY RAYMOND CARVER

SYNOPSIS

A tragic story of a road accident and a breakdown in communication which causes much pain and conflict, but ultimately ends in a reconciliation.

LIFE LESSON

The power of forgiveness and collective grief is a 'small, good thing' that can help to heal anguish and pain.

This short story was first published in Raymond Carver's 1983 collection *Cathedral*. It begins with a middle-class American couple ordering a birthday cake for their son Scotty's eighth birthday party from a local baker, who is taciturn and abrupt. Scotty is hit by a car on his way to school and although seemingly just in shock, he has a delayed reaction and later slumps into a coma. The story then centres around the painful anxiety of the parents as they have an exhausting vigil at the nearby hospital, hoping and praying that Scotty comes out of his coma. Meanwhile, the baker, without knowing Scotty's situation, embarks on a campaign of harassing late-night telephone calls to the couple as revenge over the cake he baked but which was never collected.

A Small, Good Thing is a quintessential Raymond Carver story, conveying complex human emotions in sparse and brittle prose. The agony of the couple waiting helplessly for their son to recover is beautifully rendered in a style that is neither mawkish nor melodramatic, but very emotionally affecting. Ultimately though, the story ends on a moment of hope and reconciliation. *A Small, Good Thing* is a masterful short story that condenses a whole gamut of human emotions into a tragic tale of grief.

CHAPTER 3

OPPRESSION AND CONFLICT

The title of this chapter is possibly, on the surface at least, misleading. Conflict as a theme and a device in literature can take many guises within a narrative framework, and most stories involve conflict of some form or other. In essence, conflict is defined as the clash and tension between two opposing forces, and it can be either internal or external in nature. Internal conflicts usually concern an individual who is battling against him- or herself, the internal strife brought on by chance, dilemmas, bad choices or circumstances. External conflicts find individuals struggling against forces outside of themselves, thrust into situations and forced into actions against malign powers and pressures.

Many of the novels discussed in this chapter concern external conflicts, such as wars and oppressive social and political systems (slavery, apartheid, totalitarianism) that deny people liberty and freedom. Some of the books may be regarded as protest fiction, others as providing a voice to those previously voiceless or under-represented. There are also works of literature that stand as vital records of moments in the history of humanity, and attempts to describe the seemingly indescribable.

THINGS FALL APART
BY CHINUA ACHEBE

SYNOPSIS

The struggles of Okonkwo, a tribesman in south-west Nigeria, as he battles against the destruction of his culture by the forces of Western colonialism.

LIFE LESSON

Values, customs and traditions bind communities together but are helpless in the face of change, modernization and the imposition of colonial ideas.

Published in 1958, this is the quintessential postcolonial novel, and is studied widely in schools across Africa.

Divided into three parts, the book follows the life and fate of Okonkwo, a famous wrestler and warrior of the Igbo tribe in the late nineteenth century. The first section depicts the daily lives of the Igbo and their customs, traditions, laws and superstitions over a period of three years. Okonkwo is a powerful and influential figure in the clan, but is obsessed with his masculinity and fear of showing weakness. He is prone to losing control of his violent temper. After accidentally killing a man, Okonkwo is exiled for seven years to atone for his error and appease the gods.

The following two parts cover Okonkwo's banishment and eventual return and are set against the growth of Western colonialism. Missionaries arrive and begin converting the locals to Christianity. When Okonkwo returns to his village, he finds that alongside religion, trade systems and formal education are being imposed on the native people. Friction between the old customs and the new forces of Westernization result in clashes of culture and morality as an increasingly marginalized Okonkwo watches on with a mixture of fury and despair.

An angry and often brutal novel, *Things Fall Apart* shows how traditions and cultures are diminished by colonialism in the name of progress and modernity. The British missionaries arrive with the superior belief that the Igbo are 'primitives', and make no attempt to understand Igbo religion or customs. Achebe is aware of the flaws in Igbo society – its violence and superstitions – but recognizes that the destruction and erasure of it causes a crisis in cultural identity.

Did You Know?

Things Fall Apart takes its title from the W.B. Yeats poem 'The Second Coming', which also provides the epigraph to the book. Yeats wrote the poem in 1919 in the aftermath of the First World War and at the beginning of civil war in his native Ireland — hence the poem's vivid apocalyptic tone. It is also related to the 1918-19 flu pandemic in which Yeats' wife nearly died.

INVISIBLE MAN
BY RALPH ELLISON

SYNOPSIS

The trials and tribulations of a college-educated young African American man, who, after a series of misfortunes, finds himself embroiled in the fight against racism and oppression. Gradually he finds his identity eroding and feels alienated and invisible to society.

LIFE LESSON

Divided and oppressive societies deny individuals opportunities for growth and development by stripping them of their personal identities.

Published in 1952, *Invisible Man* proved to be a watershed moment in twentieth-century African American literature. The novel is recounted in a series of recollections by a nameless ('invisible') narrator who is living underground in both a literal and metaphorical sense.

The narrator's early recollections of his life describe a clever, ambitious, if naïve young Southern black man trying to better himself in a white-dominated world. Through a series of unfortunate twists of fate and the ambivalence and antipathy of society, the narrator finds his quest for acceptance thwarted and joins the Brotherhood, an African American protest group.

Identity is a central theme in the novel, particularly the conflict and tension between how the narrator perceives himself and identities projected upon him by others: he is mistaken for somebody else several times in the book. In the end, spurned by both the black and white communities, the narrator withdraws completely, and it is then that he comes to embrace his invisible identity and feels ready to return to society.

Although often placed within the canon of twentieth-century African American fiction, Ellison refuted the suggestion that *Invisible Man* was a protest novel, and pointed out the experimental elements of the book. Ellison was a great admirer of Ernest Hemingway and William Faulkner, and wished for his work to be recognized in the broader palette of American fiction instead of being pigeonholed. There are certainly elements of Faulkner's Southern Gothic tropes in Ellison's novel, despite it being set largely in Harlem in New York. Although an often brutal book, the novel contains moments of tragicomedy and almost dream-like surrealism, stylistic devices that were uncommon in African American literature of the time.

A Chronic Case of Writer's Block?

Invisible Man was a critical and commercial success and won the prestigious National Book Award in 1953, making Ellison the first African American writer to receive the honour. On accepting the award, Ellison revealed that there were aspects of the book that he was unhappy with. He was a perfectionist: *Invisible Man* took him over five years to write and he struggled for many years on a follow-up book. Over the course of four decades he amassed more than two thousand pages of a novel with the working title of *Juneteenth*. It was never completed – a result of Ellison's obsessive perfectionism or a chronic case of writer's block – although versions were published posthumously.

SLAUGHTERHOUSE-FIVE
BY KURT VONNEGUT

SYNOPSIS

An anti-war novel detailing the adventures of Billy Pilgrim, from his early life, through his experiences of the Second World War, and then his post-war life as he struggles with post-traumatic stress disorder.

LIFE LESSON

The philosophical and moral implications of free will are negated by the unimaginable, senseless horrors of human conflict and war.

Barely two hundred pages long, *Slaughterhouse-Five* (1969) is many books simultaneously: science-fiction story, semi-autobiographical memoir, black comic satire, philosophical treatise on the meaning of life, and anti-war protest novel. The backdrop is the controversial bombing of the German city of Dresden by the Allied air forces in February 1945. Kurt Vonnegut was a prisoner of war in Dresden at the time, so he witnessed the atrocity in which an estimated 25,000 people perished, mostly civilians.

The novel begins with the words, 'All this happened, more or less …', the ambiguity signalling that the book is not a typical memoir. The narrator is unreliable and flits in and out of the action, describing his own book as being necessarily 'short and jumbled ... because there is nothing intelligent to say about a massacre'.

Having tried unsuccessfully to write about Dresden for many years, Vonnegut deploys Billy Pilgrim as a proxy for his own memories of the war. Billy has become 'unstuck in time', that is to say he can travel backwards and forwards in time, a skill afforded to him because he has embraced the philosophy of an alien race, the Tralfamadorians.

Time for the Tralfamadorians is non-linear; there is no past, present or future, there is just what there is, existing as a simultaneous whole. As a result of Billy's time travels the plot of the novel flows forwards and backwards in flashbacks and foreshadows. This non-linear structure enables Vonnegut to describe the horrors he and Billy witnessed when they emerged from the slaughterhouse in which they were being held captive during the bombing. Some critics have suggested that Billy's time travelling is a metaphor for the post-traumatic stress disorder the protagonist (and by extension Vonnegut himself) is suffering from.

Slaughterhouse-Five is an extraordinary book which works on multiple levels, by turns light and comic, angry and dark. Running through the novel is a profound sense of bewildered melancholy, as evinced by the helpless and innocent Billy Pilgrim and the novel's frequent refrain of 'so it goes'. At the beginning of the book Vonnegut recounts discussing it as an anti-war protest novel with a filmmaker, who dismissively says that he might as well write 'an anti-glacier' novel. Ultimately, Vonnegut knows his book has as much chance of stopping wars as stopping a glacier, but that does not mean we should not reflect upon the horror and human suffering that wars cause, and maybe learn something from that.

IF THIS IS A MAN
BY PRIMO LEVI

SYNOPSIS

The memoir of a Jewish Italian prisoner of war who was interned in the Nazi concentration camp at Auschwitz, Poland.

LIFE LESSON

It is redundant to attempt to find compassionate attributes in inhuman situations. In order to better understand human nature, we must bear witness to the inhuman aspects within our humanity.

Primo Levi was a member of the Italian anti-fascist resistance during the Second World War when he was captured by the fascist militia and sent to Auschwitz. Levi recalls with chilling irony that on learning of his deportation to the concentration camp he felt a sense of relief that he was going to 'a place on God's earth', and was not going to be immediately executed.

If This is a Man (1947) is a first-hand account of day-to-day life in the camp presented in a novelized format. Levi describes in dispassionate detail the camp conditions and the ritual humiliations and processes of dehumanization the inmates were forced to endure. One of the most unnerving and yet affecting aspects of the book is the air of calm and logical detachment with which Levi lists the litany of horrors in the camp. As he points out though, concepts of good and evil, persecution and justice become totally meaningless inside the barbed-wired compound.

Levi draws a metaphorical distinction between what he terms 'the drowned' and 'the saved' inside Auschwitz. 'The drowned' were inmates who, stripped of all sense of humanity, sank to 'the bottom' very quickly and perished, either through sickness, arbitrary execution or selection for the gas chambers. 'The saved' continued to survive, not necessarily because they were stronger-willed, but because they were able to gain marginal advantages (extra food or warmer clothes, for example), either through manipulations, repudiations, betrayals or theft. Levi notes how all moral and ethical imperatives were inverted inside the camp in the desperate quest for survival.

Despite its harrowing subject matter, *If This is a Man* is not entirely a gloomy book. There are moments of hope and optimism as the inmates struggle to retain the last vestiges of their humanity. In one memorable moment Levi recalls some lines from a classical poem by Dante and racks his exhausted brain to recall more, musing philosophically about how art and culture vitally enrich human life and how his memory of that poem proves he is still human. The Nazis can never strip that from him, he notes, adding that, in spite of unrelenting hunger, 'I would give up today's soup for a forgotten passage of poetry'.

THE MASTER AND MARGARITA
BY MIKHAIL BULGAKOV

SYNOPSIS

Disguised as a magician, the Devil and his
entourage visit 1930s Moscow, causing mayhem
in a society where state-sponsored atheism and
religious repression have outlawed religious beliefs.

LIFE LESSON

Good and evil can be ambiguous concepts.
Neither can exist without the other.

This novel defies characterization in terms of genre, although probably the closest description would be that it is a work of magic realism. Central to the story is a theological question of what would happen to a society where religion is banned if the Devil suddenly revealed himself in the most visible fashion. This conceit allows Bulgakov to weave in other threads concerning good and evil, salvation and redemption, authenticity and censorship in art, and the redemptive power of love.

Written at the height of Stalin's purges, *The Master and Margarita* is also a satire on the brutality and corruption of his Soviet Union. Bulgakov himself was a victim of state censorship, and at one point he asked Stalin to be allowed to leave the USSR as he could not work as a writer under such conditions.

The action alternates between 1930s Moscow (the period during which Bulgakov was writing) and Jerusalem under Pontius Pilate, who is overseeing the capture and trial of Jesus of Nazareth. The Pilate sections (later revealed to be fragments of a novel by the Master, an incarcerated writer) allow Bulgakov to discuss Christian theology. They contrast with the mayhem of the Moscow sections where the Devil, masquerading as a magician named Woland, sets about exposing the greed, materialism, bureaucracy and corruption rife in Soviet society.

The ambiguity of good and evil is skilfully foregrounded, as the novel opens with what appears to the reader to be a murder. However, Woland did not actually do the killing – he merely knew it was going to happen – and the death was actually the result of a chain of freak coincidences and choices. Likewise, the misfortunes enacted upon various other characters are as much a result of their own sinfulness and evil and the choices they make, as acts of abstract 'evil'.

A dizzyingly brilliant comic fable, the book was suppressed for many years in the USSR but developed an underground following before finally being published in full in 1967, almost three decades after Bulgakov's death.

BELOVED BY TONI MORRISON

SYNOPSIS

The story of a dysfunctional African American family haunted by their past lives as slaves and a dark family secret.

LIFE LESSON

The horrors of a traumatic past life must be acknowledged and accepted in order to move forward to a better future.

The central theme of this 1987 book is the dehumanizing effect of slavery upon individuals and communities, and how it remains a terrible stain on American history. The principal character of Sethe is a traumatized, formerly enslaved woman. A victim of rape and abuse, Sethe had fled her slave owners with her children, only to be tracked down and face the prospect of returning to slavery. In an attempt to keep her children 'free' she resolved to murder them (and presumably take her own life), but only managed to kill her youngest daughter. The house where Sethe, her daughter and partner now live is haunted by the malign spirit of this infant, and this causes her two sons to run away and abandon the family.

On returning from a day out, the family find a strange young girl, named Beloved, waiting for them. 'Beloved' was the only word that Sethe could afford to have engraved on her murdered daughter's headstone, and it is implied that this mysterious girl could be inhabited by the spirit of Sethe's dead child.

Beloved is a dark and brutal novel that uses magical realist, supernatural and Gothic elements to tell a harrowing tale of the horrors of slavery and the painful pathway to redemption. The novel is based on the true story of Margaret Garner, an escaped slave who killed her daughter to save her from being returned to slavery. The act of infanticide is a symbol of the hopeless and dehumanizing effects of slavery, but the appearance of Beloved forces the principal characters to address their trauma so that they can finally live in the present.

ONE FLEW OVER THE CUCKOO'S NEST BY KEN KESEY

SYNOPSIS

A Native American inmate of a mental institution recounts the story of a rebellious new 'patient', Randle McMurphy. McMurphy attempts to subvert the oppressive system of coercive control on the ward enforced by the tyrannical Nurse Ratched.

LIFE LESSON

Coercion and oppression are commonplace in societies that stigmatize non-conformity and difference, and suppress individuality and freedom.

This 1962 novel was inspired by Ken Kesey's experiences as a night orderly in a mental health institution in California. Drifter and con man Randle McMurphy fakes mental illness to escape being sent to a prison work farm, assuming he will be treated more leniently in hospital. The dark irony, of course, is that the institution McMurphy is sent to is run by the domineering Nurse Ratched, who oversees a regime of coercive control through psychological bullying, medication, electric shock therapy and subtle divide-and-rule manipulations. Her actions, as described by the narrator Chief Bromden, are part of what the chief sees as wider oppressive systems which he terms 'the Combine' – the collective methods in society through which individuality is crushed and conformity and passivity assured.

McMurphy quickly becomes embroiled in a power struggle with Nurse Ratched, initially to win a bet and because of his natural propensity for mischief-making. He then finds out that, unlike the fixed term of a prison sentence, he cannot be released from the ward until the hospital, and by extension Nurse Ratched, decide he is cured of his psychiatric disorder. This leaves McMurphy with a dilemma. Does he pretend to conform in order to gain his freedom or, as the figurehead of the rebellion, does he accept a degree of self-sacrifice to help 'free' his fellow patients who have been inspired by his acts of dissent?

LIFE & TIMES OF MICHAEL K
BY J.M. COETZEE

SYNOPSIS

A withdrawn and hesitant gardener embarks on an arduous journey to his mother's birthplace during a fictional civil war in South Africa's apartheid years.

LIFE LESSON

Life is often complex and throws up external pressures that are beyond comprehension or control, so it is important to appreciate simple pleasures and live life with self-possession and respect for the natural world.

Michael K is a simple gardener who sets off on a quest to take his dying mother back to her birthplace. Michael's mother dies en route, but he vows to continue the journey to return her ashes. However, *Life & Times of Michael K* (1983) is set against the backdrop of a fictitious bloody civil war, whose ravages keep disrupting his journey, leading to internment, forced labour and much hardship.

Michael K is very much an outsider. His motivations are basic: to live a life of quiet dignity at one with the earth and nature. Throughout Michael's various trials, J.M. Coetzee explores themes of personal accountability and freedom to live as one chooses. Some critics have compared this book to Franz Kafka's

The Trial, with its protagonist Josef K. Both novels depict a central character isolated and at odds with the oppressive society around them, a world of corrupt and stifling bureaucracy. Michael and his mother cannot travel without the required permit and yet this permit never arrives and cannot be applied for again – an example of a moment of Kafkaesque absurdity.

Finally, Michael concludes that his purpose in life is to be a gardener, and he was at his most content and in harmony with himself when he was tending to the land. This coincides with his belief that: 'A man must live so that he leaves no trace of his living.'

THE TIN DRUM
BY GÜNTER GRASS

SYNOPSIS

A picaresque novel in the form of the memoirs of a circus dwarf who recounts his life and adventures during the rise of Nazism, the Second World War and its aftermath.

LIFE LESSON

A philosophical allegory on the nature of guilt, responsibility and blame and a visceral critique of the grotesque absurdity of wars where survival is often more a matter of good fortune and circumstance than courage and valour.

'Granted: I am the inmate of a mental institution.' Thus begins *The Tin Drum*, with Oskar Matzerath, the narrator, slyly tipping off the reader that not everything he is going to recount in the next six hundred pages should be taken at face value. Oskar is, by his own confession, a mass of contradictions, the ultimate unreliable narrator.

This is an episodic novel where each chapter is like a macabre short story in which seemingly banal details are invested with malign significance. Grass weaves elements of fantasy, the supernatural, fairy-tale horror and satirical black humour around realistic depictions of actual historical events. The backdrop to Oskar's often grisly tales is the insidious rise of Nazism in Germany, and Grass skilfully shows how ordinary people became swept up and overcome by a collective hysteria. A bitter irony runs through the book as Grass shows the absurdity of the moral vacuum into which Germany descended under the Third Reich. This irony is often disguised in incidental details and characters such as Meyn the trumpeter, a happy drunk who 'played the trumpet too beautifully for words'. Meyn joins the SA (Nazi stormtroopers) but snaps one day and brutally murders his four beloved cats. One of Meyn's neighbours reports his deed to the authorities, who throw him out of the SA for 'conduct unbecoming for a Nazi' (burning down synagogues and lynching Jews is permissible).

The Tin Drum is a remarkable work of fiction and a deeply moral novel that addresses notions of guilt and collective responsibility. It was published in 1959 at a time when Germany was struggling to come to terms with itself in the post-war period, and contains many memorable moments that linger long in the mind. Furthermore, it a fantastic work of art that fashions wild flights of imagination from the horrors of history.

THE HANDMAID'S TALE BY MARGARET ATWOOD

SYNOPSIS

Dystopian novel depicting a totalitarian, patriarchal, quasi-religious state that strictly controls women's fertility, and maintains order through suppression of female agency and identity.

LIFE LESSON

The control of women's reproductive rights is a denial of an essential liberty and freedom.

The Handmaid's Tale (1985) depicts a dystopian future version of the USA as a society in which women are brutally subjugated under a totalitarian theocracy. The ruthless culture is observed through the eyes of the narrator Offred, one of the few remaining fertile women, known as 'handmaids'. A handmaid's role is to be a surrogate mother and procreate with members of the ruling elite, the 'Commanders'. The regime, the Republic of Gilead, uses religious fanaticism to control and oppress the population. Offred, being a woman, is denied basic rights, such as owning money or property, and young women born into the theocracy are not taught to read and write. Offred's story is narrated through present-day events and flashbacks to her life before and during the 'revolution'.

With carefully crafted details, for example the colour-coded uniforms for different social classes, and highlighting peculiar cultural features such as the popular pronouncement 'Praise be!', Atwood paints a vivid portrait of a society that has weaponized religion for political power. The gradual exposure of the horrors of life in Gilead combine with an engaging plot to drive an enthralling thriller which explores themes of gender, identity, religion and power.

Speculative Fiction or Science Fiction?

Many critics have described *The Handmaid's Tale* as a 'feminist *1984*' and Atwood herself has acknowledged the debt her novel owes to George Orwell and Aldous Huxley's *Brave New World*. However, Atwood does not like to categorize her novel (and its sequel *The Testaments*) as science fiction, preferring the term 'speculative fiction'. She argues that the former term predicts a possible future, whereas the latter term describes something which is possible in the known present.

The inspiration for the novel was Atwood's concern about the dangers to women's rights posed by the rise of right-wing religious fundamentalism in the USA during the 1980s.

HEART OF DARKNESS
BY JOSEPH CONRAD

SYNOPSIS

Classic novella about imperialism and madness,
detailing the story of Charlie Marlow, the
captain of a steamboat, who is sent up the
Congo River to find a Mr Kurtz, a rogue
colonial ivory trader who has gone missing.

LIFE LESSON

Imperialism is founded on greed, which,
rather than being a civilizing influence,
leads to an erosion of moral values.

Heart of Darkness (1899/1902) recounts Marlow's mission to find the shadowy Mr Kurtz. At first Marlow is fascinated by Kurtz, who was a very successful ivory trader and seemingly well regarded. However, he then begins to hear conflicting rumours about Kurtz and his 'illness'. When the pair finally meet, Marlow finds Kurtz has enslaved the natives of a remote village and set himself up as their tyrannical ruler.

Conrad draws a stark contrast between the supposedly civilized European society and the dark, savage continent of Africa. However, Conrad's main message is that anyone, regardless of their race or background, can be corrupted and become savages. Once some white colonials arrive in Africa, they become detached from the usual social curbs and codes of behaviour, and lose their moral values, turning to savagery to gain power and profits. As Marlow laments at one point: 'The conquest of the earth, which mostly means the taking it away from those who have a different complexion or slightly flatter noses than ourselves, is not a pretty thing when you look into it too much.'

Heart of Darkness demonstrates the disparity between the European ideal of bringing civilization to 'the natives' and the reality of it as is shown by the torture, exploitation and dehumanization of the African population. The lust for wealth and power leads to a descent into the darkness of human evil.

CATCH-22
BY JOSEPH HELLER

SYNOPSIS

A darkly comic novel examining the absurdity of war through the misadventures of an American air force bombardier and his comrades, and his increasingly desperate attempts to avoid flying dangerous missions.

LIFE LESSON

Insanity is a sane person's response to an insane world.

Published in 1961, this is the story of a group of US airmen stationed on an island off the coast of Italy during the Second World War. The principal character, Yossarian, has calculated that the probability of being killed in action increases in proportion to the number of missions undertaken. Yossarian has made the maximum number of flights required to be discharged and sent home, only for the squadron's commanders to keep arbitrarily raising the threshold.

In despair, Yossarian pleads with the squadron's medic to discharge him from service on account of insanity, only to be told of the circular reasoning that has trapped him in a predicament: airmen can be grounded if found to be insane; however, as only an insane person would fly bombing missions, asking to be excused on the grounds of insanity is the action of a rational mind and therefore proves their sanity and fitness for duty. This is 'catch-22'. Yossarian explains it with regard to his friend Orr, a pilot who keeps deliberately crashing his plane into the sea: 'Orr would be crazy to fly more missions and sane if he didn't, but if he were sane he had to fly them. If he flew them he was crazy and didn't have to, but if he didn't want to he was sane and had to.'

Throughout the novel this process of circular rationale and self-contradictory reasoning recurs to great comic effect. Catch-22 is a rule of extreme bureaucratic irrationality that is invoked to justify the outrageous actions of several people. One character attends a court martial only to find that the person prosecuting him is the same person responsible for defending him. In another incident, the arch-capitalist Milo Minderbinder makes a financial arrangement for the Germans to bomb the American base, reasoning that it was inevitably going to happen so it makes sense for him to make money out of it.

The stories, characters and events are told in a non-chronological structure, often from different perspectives, using repetition and contradiction to gradually build a wider picture of the dizzying insanity of war and the vicious absurdity of military bureaucracy.

THE BEAUTYFUL ONES ARE NOT YET BORN BY AYI KWEI ARMAH

SYNOPSIS

A man struggles to reconcile himself and his principles in the face of corruption and moral decay in postcolonial Ghana.

LIFE LESSON

It is important to maintain moral integrity and honesty even in the face of financial and material pressure, as these are values that underpin civilized societies.

Published in 1968, this story takes place in Ghana in the mid-1960s in the months leading up to the coup which ousted Kwame Nkrumah, Ghana's first elected president after independence from British colonial rule. The novel's protagonist, referred to only as 'the man', is a railway worker who struggles with his conscience, sense of responsibility and loss of faith in the face of a society that has become tainted with widespread greed and corruption. Early in the novel the man refuses a bribe at work, only to chastised by his wife for putting his principles before his responsibilities to his family. After a dinner with Koomson, a former school friend who is now a minister in Nkrumah's corrupt government, the man is offered the opportunity to take part in a dubious money-making scheme involving a fishing boat.

The stark contrast between the opulent life of his friend, who has modern luxuries and humiliates the man by refusing to use his latrine, and his struggles to adequately provide for his family torment the man with feelings of guilt and shame.

Ayi Kwei Armah populates his book with symbols of waste and decay usually related to human excrement. The man seems constantly surrounded by dirt, mould, rotting wood, grease-covered walls and human detritus. In the beginning of the novel the man falls asleep on a bus and dribbles on the seat; the conductor ejects the man and the bus driver spits on him. This emphasis on scatological details and filth acts as a powerful symbol for the rotten, corrupt core of Nkrumah's regime.

The Beautyful Ones Are Not Yet Born is an indictment of how societies freed from oppression can quickly squander that freedom by being seduced by greed and corruption. Although bleak in its outlook, at the end of the book the man sees the title of the novel sprayed as a slogan on the side of a bus and feels that, now the government has fallen, there is perhaps still some hope for the future.

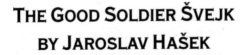

THE GOOD SOLDIER ŠVEJK
BY JAROSLAV HAŠEK

SYNOPSIS

Satirical episodic novel detailing the misadventures
of a good-natured, although simple-minded,
soldier drafted into the Austro–Hungarian
army during the First World War.

LIFE LESSON

War is stupid and futile; the Catholic Church can
be hypocritical; military bureaucracy can be absurd.

The Czech writer Jaroslav Hašek planned this comic novel
to have six volumes. But, a notorious hedonist and drinker,
he died suddenly of a heart attack at the age of thirty-nine
in 1923, the year the fourth volume was published. The
inspiration for *The Good Soldier Švejk* came from Hašek's
own experiences serving on the Eastern Front during the First
World War.

At the heart of the novel is a deeply ironic contradiction.
Many Czech nationals in the Habsburg Empire felt
considerable animosity to Austrian rule, viewing Austrians
and Hungarians as enemies and oppressors. This situation
was exacerbated during the First World War when Czechs
were conscripted into the Austro–Hungarian army and were

forced to fight for their enemy in a war they did not start, did not want and did not understand. Hašek turns this absurd fait accompli on its head by having his character of Švejk manically enthusiastic about fighting in the war and volunteering despite being previously discharged from the army due to being considered too 'dim-witted'.

The novel is full of comic episodes highlighting military incompetence, and the accident-prone Švejk manages to constantly be a thorn in the side of army authorities while maintaining a persona of cheerful idiocy. The reader is left to decide if Švejk really is an imbecile, or if he is executing a carefully thought-out plan of subversion by feigning stupidity – the ultimate act of passive aggression. A very funny novel which is considered to be one of the first anti-war satires, Hašek's masterpiece was acknowledged by Joseph Heller as having a major influence on Heller's novel *Catch-22*.

GERMINAL BY EMILE ZOLA

SYNOPSIS

The story of a migrant worker in northern France in the 1880s who takes a job as a miner and experiences appalling exploitation and working conditions. These inspire him to lead an ill-fated workers' revolt.

LIFE LESSON

Hope, resilience and solidarity are vital forces
of resistance in any struggle against oppressive
systems of power and exploitation.

This is the thirteenth book in Emile Zola's epic series of twenty
novels, known collectively as the *Les Rougon-Macquart*, which
recount the history of two families in nineteenth-century
France. Published in 1885, *Germinal* details the struggles of
Étienne Lantier, an idealistic young man who takes a job as a
miner in a small town. Étienne is appalled by the conditions
in which the miners are forced to live and work. He meets
Souvarine, a Russian anarchist and political agitator who
espouses revolutionary rhetoric and inspires Étienne to adopt
socialist principles.

Étienne seems to have inherited the hot-headed impulsiveness
that is a common character trait in members of the Macquart
family (genetic characteristics is a recurrent aspect in Zola's cycle
of novels). As conditions for the miners deteriorate and the pit
company finds increasingly cruel ways to dock the miners' pay,
Étienne finds himself rousing the miners to strike action that
escalates with devastating and destructive consequences.

Zola skilfully contrasts the poverty and deprivation
of the miners with the affluence of the capitalist class, and
paints a vivid portrait of the miners' struggle to survive in
conditions akin to slavery. *Germinal* is widely considered to be
Zola's masterpiece and caused a sensation upon publication.
Although the miners' insurrection ultimately proves to be
fruitless, Zola ends the novel with a message of hope for future
change which has been often quoted in support of socialist

causes across the world:

> *'Beneath the blazing of the sun, in that morning of new growth, the countryside rang with song, as its belly swelled with a black and avenging army of men, germinating slowly in its furrows, growing upwards in readiness for harvests to come, until one day soon their ripening would burst open the earth itself.'*

Did You Know?

After *Germinal* was published, Zola found himself under attack from both sides of the political spectrum. Conservatives accused him of exaggerating the conditions of the miners. Socialists criticized the novel's depiction of the working class as patronizing and crass. Zola furiously refuted these criticisms by pointing to the extensive research he had undertaken. He had made frequent visits to the area where the novel is set, conducted interviews with miners, and had tricked his way into the mines to see working conditions with his own eyes. During one of his visits, Zola also witnessed a riot by striking miners which provided the basis for one of the most dramatic moments in the novel.

GRAVITY'S RAINBOW
BY THOMAS PYNCHON

SYNOPSIS

Sprawling satirical science-fiction novel concerning the development of missile technology at the end of the Second World War and its aftermath.

LIFE LESSON

The corrupting influence of political power upon technological advances could have grave consequences for humankind.

This 1973 novel comprises multiple plot lines and switches in narrative voice that gradually converge around the quest to uncover a legendary German missile towards the end of the Second World War. The principal character is a hapless American intelligence operative, Tyrone Slothrop, who discovers that his sexual arousal and carnal trysts take place at the sites of future German V-2 missile strikes in London.

For Pynchon, the use of technology and the development and expansion of the military-industrial complex after the Second World War presented a clear threat to the future of humanity. He mixes historical facts, science, conspiracy theories, popular culture and distinctly lowbrow humour to satirize the absurdity of the arms race. Mental illness and paranoia are also explored throughout the novel. The increasingly unreliable narrators make it difficult to determine how much of what is described is actually happening, and how much of it is a product of psychosis and delusional hallucination. Paranoia was, of course, the bedrock of the post-war arms race, driving the feverish appetite for bigger and ever more destructive weapons.

The novel begins with an epigraph from an essay by Wernher von Braun, a Nazi rocket scientist and co-inventor of the V-2 rocket, who was co-opted by American intelligence after the war and worked for NASA. Giving the example of the extinction of the dinosaurs, when semblances of their ecosystem survived and were reborn, Von Braun argues that, 'Nature does not know extinction. All it knows is transformation!' Pynchon seems to suggest that rocket scientists and the military-industrial complex share this chilling view of human annihilation.

BRAVE NEW WORLD
BY ALDOUS HUXLEY

SYNOPSIS

Dystopian science-fiction novel set in a technocratic, future society known as World State in which emotions and individuality are conditioned out of people from birth. Humans are bred into a particular class according to their utilitarian value.

LIFE LESSON

It is dangerous to allow the state to control new technology, particularly genetic technology. Capitalism and industrialization can suppress individuality and erode human culture.

The 'brave new world' of this 1932 novel maintains social stability through the manipulation and application of technological systems of control. Human beings are cloned as specific types (Alpha, Beta, Gamma, Delta or Epsilon) to fulfil certain roles in society, and are neurologically programmed to accept their jobs and status without question. The population is kept in a constant state of passivity by a soothing narcotic substance named soma, which induces artificial feelings of peace and happiness.

The plot concerns a psychologist, Bernard, a member of the Alpha group who has become disillusioned and critical of the World State and its rigid social controls. While on holiday, Bernard and his girlfriend Lenina visit a Savage Reservation, an area outside of World State, and witness things that have been eradicated or repressed in their society such as natural birth, religion, rituals and diseases. There they encounter a woman named Linda who was originally from World State, but was marooned on the reservation after becoming illegally pregnant. Linda has a grown-up son John, who, having been born outside of World State, has not been subjected to neurological programming and social conditioning, and so has raw human emotions and instincts. Bernard takes Linda and John back to World State, where the 'natural savage' John is an object of prurient fascination, becoming something of a celebrity. A conflict arises between John's natural thoughts, emotions and passions, and the soulless, emotionless values of the society he has been transplanted into. Huxley's novel provided a blueprint for future dystopian novels (see also *1984* and *The Handmaid's Tale*), and its doubts about the ethics of genetic technology are as chillingly relevant today as they were in the 1930s.

THE COLOR PURPLE
BY ALICE WALKER

SYNOPSIS

The story of a young African American girl who endures a life of hardship and abuse, but gradually gains confidence and strength on her long journey to self-realization and independence.

LIFE LESSON

Faith and perseverance can help us to draw strength from adversity. Love and friendship can keep people going in times of trouble, and forgiveness can help overcome past hurts.

This epistolary novel recounts the harrowing story of Celie, who, from the age of fourteen, writes letters to God to describe her life and her relationships. Having given birth to two children after being raped by her father, and then coerced into an abusive marriage, Celie struggles with the trauma and loneliness of her life. Her only respite comes from her loving relationship with her younger sister Nettie. Nettie goes to Africa to do missionary work, leaving Celie even more isolated and trapped. When Shug Avery, a charismatic blues singer (and mistress of Celie's husband) joins the household, Celie experiences a sexual awakening that leads her on a path of self-discovery and freedom. Alongside Celie's account there is a dual narrative in the letters from Nettie recounting her experiences in Africa, letters which Celie's husband has been hiding from her.

The Color Purple weaves themes of race, sexism, religion, gender roles, power, identity and imperialism into a multi-faceted story of female friendship, love and solidarity. The novel was awarded the Pulitzer Prize for fiction in 1983, the year after its publication, making Alice Walker the first woman of colour to receive the accolade. It was adapted into an Oscar-winning film directed by Steven Spielberg, and has also been turned into a successful Broadway musical.

THE LOTTERY IN BABYLON
BY JORGE LUIS BORGES

SYNOPSIS

Dystopian short story set in a mythical country named Babylon, which has been governed for centuries by a lottery system administered by a shadowy corporation known only as 'the Company'.

LIFE LESSON

Totalitarian regimes suppress and control
individuals. Chance has a major role to
play in matters of human agency.

This short story was published in Argentinian writer Jorge
Luis Borges' celebrated 1941 collection *The Garden of Forking
Paths*. The story describes a fictitious country called Babylon
where a lottery holds a malign and controlling influence over
the population.

Originally the lottery was a simple raffle-like system, offering
a financial prize. Over time, however, the lottery began to exert
more and more control over people's lives. Although prizes were
still awarded for winning tickets, the Company, the shadowy
organisation that administers the lottery, instigated fines and
punishments for 'unlucky' tickets. Eventually, participation in
the lottery is made compulsory to all (apart from a small elite),
and every aspect of individual free will is subsequently reduced
to a matter of pure chance.

The Lottery in Babylon displays Borges' talent for blending
fantasy, satire and magic realism into a cautionary tale warning
against state-sponsored interventions in people's lives, no
matter how benign they may appear to be.

CHAPTER 4

PSYCHOLOGY AND IDENTITY

This chapter concerns what may be deemed psychological novels, works of fiction that bring to the forefront the thoughts, feelings, emotions and motivations of characters, and explore how these shape external actions and events. It is often considered that psychological novels came to prominence in twentieth-century fiction, when modernist writers such as James Joyce, Joseph Conrad and Virginia Woolf began to experiment with different literary forms and devices such as interior monologues, streams of consciousness, and multiple or shifting authorial voices and perspectives. The works of psychoanalysts such as Sigmund Freud and Carl Jung influenced these authors as they sought new ways to express human experiences in fiction.

Psychological perspectives in fiction can, however, be traced back further than the twentieth century. Early novels in English such as Samuel Richardson's *Pamela* (1740) and Laurence Sterne's *Tristram Shandy* (1759) used literary techniques which examined the thoughts and feelings of their protagonists. Sterne's novel is often cited as one of the earliest examples of stream of consciousness writing in fiction. Other writers who had a profound influence on the modern psychological novel include Fyodor Dostoevsky and Knut Hamsun, who were particularly concerned with human consciousness and identity.

DON QUIXOTE
BY MIGUEL DE CERVANTES

SYNOPSIS

Classic of seventeenth-century literature detailing
the misadventures of a deluded minor member
of the Spanish nobility who imagines he is a
knight errant on a quest to restore the virtues
of chivalry to a cruel and cynical world.

LIFE LESSON

Life is a challenge and an individual who believes
in values of goodness should strive to make
life as it could be, not accept life as it is.

The Ingenious Gentleman Don Quixote of La Mancha (to give it its full title) was published in two parts in 1605 and 1615, and is often cited as the first modern European novel. There are many reasons for this, particularly Cervantes' innovative use of an array of literary devices which have influenced generations of writers for four centuries. The basic plot concerns Alonso Quijano, an aged, untitled aristocrat and bibliophile who has become so enamoured with chivalric romances that he deludes himself that he is a 'knight errant' on a quest to promote the noble values of chivalry. In order to live out his fantasies, he changes his name to Don Quixote and sets out on his mission.

Around the conceit of Quijano's 'madness', Cervantes weaves a series of stories of his protagonist's quests and the characters he meets on his journeys. The novel, as alluded to above, deploys many contemporary literary devices such as a highly unreliable narrator, shifting perspectives, digressions, and stories within stories. The tragic 'joke', of course, is that Quijano is the only person who believes he is noble and chivalrous; all the characters he encounters (with the exception of his 'squire' Sancho Panza) ridicule and cruelly exploit Quixote.

Don Quixote explores many themes, from the disconnect between fantasy and reality, sanity versus insanity, the class structure of medieval Europe, and questions of identity and self-creation, to name but a few. It is impossible not to identify with Don Quixote's pursuit to, in the words of a song from the musical *Man of La Mancha*, 'dream the impossible dream'.

Did You Know?

Miguel de Cervantes was a decorated soldier under the Spanish Crown and fought for Pope Pious V's Holy League against the Ottoman Empire. In 1575, he and his brother Rodrygo were captured by the Ottomans, with a ransom set for their release. Cervantes' family could only afford to pay for one brother and chose to free Rodrygo, leaving Miguel in captivity for five years. In the section of *Don Quixote* known as 'The Captive's Tale', a passing mention is given to 'a Spanish soldier named something de Saavedra'. Cervantes' full name was Miguel de Cervantes Saavedra, so this is one of many examples where the author intrudes in his own narrative.

THE HEART OF THE MATTER
BY GRAHAM GREENE

SYNOPSIS

A married British police officer in colonial West Africa during the Second World War begins an affair with a young woman. The affair forces him into a moral dilemma and to question his faith as his life unravels.

LIFE LESSON

To what extent are individuals responsible for the happiness of others? What are the limits of Christian faith when confronted with complex moral dilemmas?

This 1948 novel is the story of Henry Scobie, a police officer protecting a small expat community in Africa. Trapped in a loveless marriage, Scobie is a devout Catholic who is racked with guilt over his wife's unhappiness and the death of their only child some years previously. His wife Louise wishes to escape to South Africa, and, having been passed over for promotion, Scobie is forced to take a loan from a local black marketeer in order to pay for Louise's passage. Scobie then meets a young, traumatized widow and begins a passionate affair that sets off a chain of events leading to tragedy.

As with many of Graham Greene's novels, the Catholic faith is a central theme. There are discussions of Catholic theology throughout the book as Scobie struggles to navigate a series of emotionally charged moral predicaments and wrestles with guilt, pity, damnation and salvation.

The Heart of the Matter is a claustrophobic novel where the setting provides a metaphorical backdrop to its central themes. There are frequent descriptions of the stifling and oppressive climate, the heat and humidity foreshadowing the fires of damnation into which Scobie is descending. Ultimately, Scobie, despite his best intentions, is undone by the sin of pride and the burden of pity: 'It seemed to Scobie later that this was the ultimate border he had reached in happiness: being in darkness, alone, with the rain falling, without love or pity.'

OBLOMOV BY IVAN GONCHAROV

SYNOPSIS

Nineteenth-century Russian novel depicting
the life of a nobleman who is pathologically
incapable of making any decisions. He lives a life
of idle inertia, the definitive 'superfluous man'.

LIFE LESSON

There is no moral imperative to act as others do.
Life is composed of many seemingly important
decisions and actions which, when viewed
in isolation, are petty and meaningless.

Oblomov (1859) is the quintessential example of the 'superfluous man' novel, a key literary trope in nineteenth-century Russian literature (see also *A Hero of Our Time*). Ilya Ilyitch Oblomov is a wealthy and educated Russian aristocrat who spends his days either lying in bed or lazing in a chair, fretting about the petty minutiae of everyday life. The merest disturbance to his life of perpetual idleness and slumber causes him deep distress. Oblomov's sincerest hope is that by ignoring a problem it may just disappear.

There is little actual action: Oblomov spends the first one hundred and fifty pages in bed. He is, however, visited by various friends and acquaintances, whose busy lives and problems do

Oblomov Gets Spiked

Oblomov was adapted into a play by Italian writer Riccardo Aragno. In 1964, British comedian Spike Milligan, a big fan of Goncharov's novel, bought the rights to Aragno's adaptation and, wanting to take on serious roles, arranged a production in London. On the opening night, however, Milligan had a panic attack and forgot many of his lines. In an attempt to salvage the disaster, he reverted to what he knew best, manic and anarchic improvised comedy. Although savaged by critics, Milligan continued to use *Oblomov* as a vehicle for comedy improvisation, spontaneously rewriting the play every night. He would argue with the audience, start the play sitting in the theatre's circle, wear false limbs, and refer to cast members by their real names. On one occasion Milligan spotted that his fellow *Goon Show* comedian and friend Peter Sellers was in the royal box as a guest of Queen Elizabeth II. Milligan broke off the play and launched into a two-way improvisation with Sellers which lasted several minutes. The show proved a big hit with audiences. It was renamed *Son of Oblomov*, since it now bore little resemblance to Aragno's script.

little to inspire Oblomov, and merely confirm to him that he is better off doing nothing.

Oblomov is a unique novel, and although on the surface nothing much really happens over six hundred or so pages, the book is never dull. The reader is drawn into Oblomov's world, into his thoughts and musings, his paranoia, neurosis and dreams. The book drifts along in a languid, sleepy way that perfectly reflects the character of its anti-hero. Ostensibly a satire on the decaying Russian aristocracy, modern scholars have focused on the psychological aspects of the novel and in particular Oblomov's depression caused by the tedium of modern life, or as Oblomov puts it: 'Life, it gets at you at every turn, it just won't leave you alone.'

THE BELL JAR
BY SYLVIA PLATH

SYNOPSIS

A semi-autobiographical novel detailing the life of a talented young writer as she struggles with mental health issues and her sense of selfhood.

LIFE LESSON

A withering critique of society's expectations of, and attitudes towards, independently minded, ambitious women in the 1950s.

The only novel written by American poet Sylvia Plath, this is a *roman à clef* ('novel with a key') – a form identified in French literature as real experiences concealed behind the disguise of a fictional world. It relates the life of Esther Greenwood, a gifted student who wins a prestigious internship at a New York fashion magazine. Esther feels increasingly alienated from the seemingly superficial world around her and starts to sink into suffocating bouts of anxiety, depression and ultimately suicidal thinking. She undergoes a series of 'treatments', including electroshock therapy.

There is a dark legacy behind Plath's frank and honest description of a young woman's struggles with mental health: Plath took her own life shortly after the novel was published in 1963. However, there is much in *The Bell Jar* that is comic and acerbic in tone. Esther's musings and self-reflections are laced with delicious irony and at times come to resemble a series of clever epigrams, for example: 'The trouble was, I had been inadequate all along, I simply hadn't thought about it.'

An unusual novel, *The Bell Jar* contains a good deal of insight into the pressures to conform to a certain ideal of middle-class womanhood in America after the Second World War. Moreover, it explores how society drains individuals of their sense of self-determinism: 'To the person in the bell jar, blank and stopped as a dead baby, the world itself is the bad dream.'

L'ÉTRANGER
BY ALBERT CAMUS

SYNOPSIS

A disaffected man, insensible to the feelings
and emotions of the people around him,
commits a senseless murder for which
he shows no guilt or remorse.

LIFE LESSON

A demonstration of the absurdity of
searching for meaning in life where there is
no higher meaning or order to the world.

Published in English as *The Outsider* or *The Stranger*, this is
usually considered to be an existential novel that explores
the futility of searching for meaning in life. It follows the
story of Meursault, a man who is curiously detached from
the feelings and emotions of the people around him, as he
becomes drawn into a feud that Raymond, an acquaintance,
is having with an ex-girlfriend and her family. After an
altercation on a beach during which Raymond is slashed,
Meursault returns to the beach armed with a pistol and
confronts one of Raymond's assailants before shooting
the man dead. The rest of the novel concerns Meursault's
incarceration and trial as he struggles to come to any rational

Did You Know?

The word *L'Étranger* in French has several related but distinct meanings. It can describe someone living in a foreign country (Meursault is a French colonial living in Algeria), an individual alienated from society, or an isolated traveller. The novel has always been published as *The Outsider* in the UK and *The Stranger* in the USA. This is not due to a quibble over the correct translation, but to a breakdown in communication. The first English translation was planned as *The Stranger*, but a British publisher had recently published *Cudzoziemka*, a Polish novel by Maria Kuncewiczowa, as *The Stranger*, so in Britain Camus' book was changed to *The Outsider*. Unfortunately, the US publishers who shared the translation rights were not informed of the title change before the novel went to print, hence the different titles.

explanation or understanding of the murder he committed and its implications.

Camus rejected the description of his novel as existential fiction, partly because he disliked the label and partly through a distrust of 'armchair philosophy'. Although there are clear aspects of existentialism apparent in the book, and intellectual nihilism was very much in vogue at the time, modern critics have focused on an alternative interpretation.

Meursault's total lack of empathy or understanding for the feelings of others, his emotional detachment and his hypersensitivity to heat, light and sounds are consistent with autism spectrum disorders such as Asperger's syndrome. Little was known of autism at the time of *L'Étranger's* publication in 1942, and it would be several years before Asperger's was formally diagnosed. However, it is thought Camus modelled the character of Meursault on an acquaintance who exhibited peculiar anti-social traits consistent with Asperger's. It is possible, therefore, that rather than presenting a diatribe on the futility of looking for meaning in life, Camus has inadvertently given a powerful portrait of autism, encapsulated by the novel's opening line: 'Mother died today. Or yesterday maybe, I don't know.'

No Longer Human
by Osamu Dazai

Synopsis

A semi-autobiographical novel following the life of a deeply disaffected young Japanese man from childhood, through his education and adolescence to adulthood, as he descends into depression and self-destruction.

LIFE LESSON

An inability to identify with one's sense
of self and feeling forced to live in bad
faith to gain acceptance from society leads
to depression and social alienation.

No Longer Human is presented as notebooks or journals detailing the life and thoughts of a young Japanese man named Ōba Yōzō. The notebooks have been found by an unnamed writer/editor who provides a foreword and an afterword that bookend the novel.

The life of Ōba Yōzō is told in three separate parts described as memoranda, with each part relating to a specific period of trauma and psychological disturbance in Ōba's short life. The first memorandum finds the child Ōba struggling to relate to life and feeling a profound sense of alienation and otherness. In order to forge relations with others and stave off his crushing feelings of loneliness, Ōba adopts a clownish persona but internally chastises himself for being a fraud. Ōba is indecently assaulted but decides to keep the abuse secret for fear of not being believed.

The second and third memoranda cover Ōba as a young adult and detail his slide into despair and self-destructive cycles. Riddled with self-doubt and drinking heavily, Ōba neglects his studies as an artist and is expelled from university. He embarks upon a series of doomed and inappropriate relationships with women, one of which ends in a failed suicide pact, leaving Ōba overcome with guilt and self-disgust. For a brief time he has a positive relationship with a young woman who helps him to stop drinking, but an old friend coming back into his life sees him descend once again into depression and self-destruction. Published in 1948, this unsettling portrayal of social alienation, loneliness and depression is one of the masterworks of twentieth-century Japanese literature.

TRISTRAM SHANDY
BY LAURENCE STERNE

SYNOPSIS

A sprawling, comic, fake autobiography about the life of the eponymous gentleman and his family and acquaintances.

LIFE LESSON

'All I wish is, that it may be a lesson to the world, "to let people tell their stories in their own way."' – Tristram Shandy

Published in 1759, this episodic comic novel is credited with introducing different forms of experimental writing. Sterne deploys a stream of consciousness technique, self-conscious narration, and passages of direct address between author and reader to reimagine and redraw the possibilities of the novel form.

Although supposedly an autobiography, Sterne deliberately subverts that by starting Tristram's story before he was actually conceived. Sterne also inverts another classical narrative form, the Homeric pattern of constructing an epic in the middle of a chronological sequence, and then reflecting backwards to flesh out details and causal effects which impact upon future story developments. Instead, Tristram Shandy, as narrator, finds it impossible to describe anything directly without wild diversions into his 'opinions'. Consequently, two and a half volumes pass with background information and digressions which may or may not be relevant (but provide Sterne with ample scope to flex his satiric wit) before the titular character is even born.

Sterne was greatly influenced by the medieval French satirist François Rabelais (see *Gargantua and Pantagruel*) and shares his French counterpart's fascination with scatological humour and human bodies. In one incident the child Tristram is accidentally circumcised while urinating out of a window. Noses are a central theme throughout the novel on account of Tristram's father's belief that a prominent and shapely nose is a prerequisite for a successful life (Tristram's nose is mangled during birth). Sterne directly acknowledges the influence of Rabelais (and Cervantes' *Don Quixote*) by actually borrowing and rearranging whole sections of Rabelais' texts within his own narrative to illuminate comic effects. *Tristram Shandy* is not an easy book to read – the digressions make it deliberately difficult – but it remains a highly influential work that invented experimental fiction and alternative comedy with its core message to 'let people tell their stories in their own way'.

THE ADVENTURES OF AUGIE MARCH
BY SAUL BELLOW

SYNOPSIS

Picaresque novel following the life of an
impoverished young Jewish boy growing up
in Chicago during the Great Depression, and
his struggles to make his way in the world.

LIFE LESSON

Do not allow the influence of others
to determine your own fate, but forge
your own path in the world.

In classical literature the picaro is a likeable rogue, usually of
humble origins, who journeys through life living by his or
her wits. A common feature of picaresque novels is a series of
situations and episodes that the principal character navigates
between in a freewheeling fashion. Augie March is a typical picaro,
and this 1953 book follows his escapades through life, with his
'adventures' centring around the various jobs he undertakes in
order to survive, and his relationships with women and his family.

Born to a poor, disadvantaged family in a rough area of
Chicago, Augie has no father and a mother who is losing her
eyesight. The only guidance he receives in life comes from a
tyrannical Jewish matriarch called Grandmother (who is not

a blood relative). In many ways Augie represents the opposite of the American Dream, for although he strives for success, he never quite achieves his aims, and finds himself having to start over again or being pulled back to his origins. Many of the people Augie encounters attempt to manipulate him in various schemes, some of which skirt on the edges of criminality or are morally questionable. However, he somehow manages to scrape by and lives to fight on, still chasing the dream.

At the end of the novel Augie philosophizes about the nature of failure and decides that it is the journey to self-realization that is important, not the destination.

<hr />

THE CATCHER IN THE RYE
BY J.D. SALINGER

SYNOPSIS

Episodic novel recounting the events of two days in the life of a disaffected youth, Holden Caulfield, as he wanders around New York following his expulsion from school.

LIFE LESSON

It is important to maintain strong connections with people in order to face the problems life throws at you. Running away from problems only exacerbates them.

On the surface, the narrator and protagonist of *The Catcher in the Rye* (1951) is the prototype 'rebel without a cause'. Holden Caulfield is from a wealthy, middle-class background. He is intelligent and articulate, and attends a notable private school. Beneath the veneer of privilege, however, lies a very angry and depressed adolescent struggling with his progress into adulthood.

The novel opens with Holden looking back at what he has come to identify as a pivotal point in his descent into mental exhaustion. After being expelled from school through apathy and lack of application, Holden spends a weekend in New York and undertakes a series of casual encounters in an attempt to make a meaningful connection with someone.

Although *The Catcher in the Rye* was initially conceived as an adult book, it is popular among adolescents for its depiction of adolescent angst and teenage alienation. Young adults identify with Holden's struggles and his rebellious nature.

Holden rails against 'phony' (superficial) people and situations and is searching for something which he cannot articulate. One of the keys to his state of mind is that he is suffering from depression and post-traumatic stress disorder. Two incidents in Holden's past are alluded to: the death from leukaemia of his younger brother Allie and the suicide of one of his classmates. The words 'depression' or 'depressing' are mentioned more than forty times in Holden's thoughts and observations.

Although *The Catcher in the Rye* can be read as a 'coming of age' novel that covers themes such as identity, loss of innocence, grief and sexual awakening, it is also a vivid portrayal of mental health issues that are becoming increasingly prevalent among young people. If there is one lesson that the novel illuminates, it is that young people cannot face their problems alone; they need support and understanding.

HUNGER BY KNUT HAMSUN

SYNOPSIS

An impoverished young writer wanders around the streets of Oslo in a state of mental and physical distress. He has a series of encounters with people as he searches for food and shelter.

LIFE LESSON

A novel exploring the conflict between the individual and society and how isolated individuals react to the experience of psychological and physical oppression caused through poverty and starvation.

Published in 1890, *Hunger* is often cited as the first existential novel and a precursor to twentieth-century psychological novels. The plot, such as there is, takes place entirely in the mind of an unnamed struggling writer as he wanders the city of Kristiania (now Oslo), and the book takes the form of stream of consciousness monologues.

Hunger becomes central to the narrator's motivations in both a literal and a metaphorical sense. He details his sense of disorientation, pain and fatigue as he endures the effects of starvation on the body and mind. On another level, the concept of emptiness is used as a criticism of modernity and urban isolation, as many of the people the narrator encounters are alone, disaffected and needy.

Hunger also points metaphorically to the smothering strictures in which all people can become trapped. The narrator has chosen to place himself outside of society, believing he is above other people. He is also plagued by vanity and self-importance, and several times, out of pride, conceals his desperate situation or undertakes irrational acts of generosity that are a detriment to his own health and well-being.

This is an uncomfortable book to read, particularly the descriptions of the effects of starvation on the body. The novel is thought to be semi-autobiographical, based upon Hamsun's struggles as a fledgling writer trying to make a living.

PAMELA BY SAMUEL RICHARDSON

SYNOPSIS

An epistolary novel consisting of letters and journal entries from a young maidservant Pamela Andrews who, after the death of her mistress, finds herself the object of unwanted and inappropriate sexual advances by her new master.

LIFE LESSON

Sticking to a moral code and being true to one's
beliefs will eventually have its just rewards.

Pamela; or, Virtue Rewarded (1740) recounts the life of a
pretty young servant girl, first through a series of letters and
later through journal entries, all of which are addressed to her
parents. On the death of her mistress, Mrs B, Pamela enters
into the service of the heir to the estate, Mr B.

Mr B embarks upon a prolonged attempt to seduce Pamela,
at first showering her with gifts but moving on to ever more
desperate measures as his attentions are rebuffed. After a
series of abuses including voyeurism, bribery, sexual assaults
and kidnapping all fail to sully Pamela's virtue, Mr B comes
to realize the distress he has caused and becomes a reformed
character. He repents, and agrees to relinquish his control over
her and let her return to her family.

On receiving a letter from Mr B apologizing for his sinful
behaviour and begging for her forgiveness, Pamela is overcome
with a sense of melancholy and realizes she has fallen in love.
When Mr B falls ill, Pamela returns to nurse him and on his
recovery accepts his proposal of marriage.

Pamela is one of the earliest novels to explore a character's
psyche – their inner thoughts and emotions. At its time, it
was considerably subversive with its depiction of the English
class system and inter-class marriage, the latter receiving
much criticism. It is also the first novel to deal with domestic
abuse, sexual assault and male coercive control of women.
Richardson's actual views on these issues appears ambiguous.
It seems likely that Richardson believed he was writing a form

of 'conduct book', a popular genre at the time which consisted of pseudo self-help manuals providing guidance on virtues, manners and moral behaviour.

Crime and Punishment
by Fyodor Dostoevsky

Synopsis

A penniless former student plans and commits what he regards as a justifiable murder as a means of demonstrating his intellectual and moral superiority over others.

Life Lesson

The rationalization of morality and ethics is futile as it does not reflect the complexity of the human mind nor address emotional concepts such as guilt, responsibility and justice.

This is the story of Rodion Raskolnikov, an impoverished and troubled young man who murders an unscrupulous pawnbroker. Raskolnikov rationalizes the murder on the grounds that he is morally and intellectually superior to his victim. He also plans to rob the woman. This provides a second utilitarian justification for his crime, as he can use the money, which the woman has leeched from other people's poverty and desperation, to do great things.

After committing the murder, Raskolnikov is gripped by psychological trauma and emotional anguish that manifests itself in feverish paranoia as he grapples with the internal and external consequences of his crime.

Raskolnikov is one of Dostoevsky's most memorable and complex creations. To some degree he displays all the symptoms of being a sociopath, with his superiority complex, narcissism and belief that he can commit whatever acts he desires without compunction. However, despite his nihilistic protestations, Raskolnikov is prone to acts of kindness and generosity, and has a genuine empathy for the suffering of others who are oppressed and struggling through no fault of their own.

The main inspiration for *Crime and Punishment*, which was published in 1867, was Dostoevsky's distrust of radical movements in contemporary Russian intellectual circles. He uses the character of Raskolnikov to illustrate what he saw as the dangers of taking fashionable 'Western' trends in philosophy, such as rationalism and utilitarianism, to their extremes. For Dostoevsky, rationalism, although in principle a test of truth, suppressed spontaneous Christian emotions such as empathy and compassion. So, in *Crime and Punishment* he shows this conflict in Raskolnikov's actions, fall and eventual redemption.

A WILD SHEEP CHASE
BY HARUKI MURAKAMI

SYNOPSIS

Surreal pseudo-detective story concerning
a quest to find a wandering spirit, currently
embodied in a mystical sheep, that grants the
person it inhabits supernatural powers.

LIFE LESSON

Emotional growth can lead to understanding
and accepting one's true identity.

The third book in a loose sequence of novels known as 'The
Trilogy of the Rat', this novel continues the adventures of a
nameless narrator and his friend known as 'the Rat'. Published
in 1982, the book can, however, be read as a standalone
work without familiarity with the two previous novels in the
sequence: *Pinball* (1973) and *Hear the Wind Sing* (1979).

A Wild Sheep Chase marks a notable departure for Murakami
in terms of style and genre. Whereas the two previous novels
in the sequence were realistic and reflective in tone and voice,
Murakami's third novel develops a genre-mashing mix of
surrealism, mysticism and the absurd that has become the
trademark of his later works.

The plot is part detective fiction, part mystical quest as the narrator is sent on a mission to find a sheep which is possessed by a supernatural spirit that can inhabit the souls of human beings and bestow special powers upon them. Through dream-like hallucinations, wild plot diversions, inner monologues and philosophical reflections, Murakami presents the search for the sheep as a journey towards self-realization and acceptance of loss.

The novel defies classification as it mixes East Asian folklore with hardboiled thriller tropes, science fiction, deadpan humour and mysticism. Murakami's fiction shares similar DNA with the work of Kurt Vonnegut (see *Slaughterhouse-Five*), another gleeful subverter of literary forms and an acknowledged influence upon Murakami's work, although culturally Murakami's novels are also in the tradition of Japanese manga comics and anime.

A Wild Sheep Chase is considered to be the first work of Murakami's 'mature fiction' and a good entry-level novel to explore his wild and abstract view of modern Japanese society.

THE PICTURE OF DORIAN GRAY
BY OSCAR WILDE

SYNOPSIS

A Gothic tale of an impressionable young aesthete who purchases eternal youth and beauty at the expense of his soul, which becomes corrupted by his life of hedonism and amorality.

LIFE LESSON

A life of selfishness, vanity and excess will
lead to unhappiness and self-destruction.

At the start of this novel, the artist Basil Hallward paints a beautiful portrait of the handsome young man Dorian Gray which encapsulates Dorian's youth and vitality. On seeing the picture, Dorian comments that he wishes he could trade places with the portrait and that his picture would age and lose its beauty, whereas he would remain forever youthful.

His wish is granted. Dorian then embarks upon a life devoted to hedonistic pleasures. He falls in love with a young actress named Sibyl Vane, who is totally besotted with him, and they become engaged to marry. However, Sibyl's love for Dorian is so all-consuming that her acting ability deserts her. Dorian then cruelly rejects Sibyl, stating that her acting was what he found attractive, and bereft of that she means nothing to him. On returning home, Dorian notices that the expression on the face of his portrait has changed to a harsh sneer. Recognizing the correlation between his actions and the image on the painting, Dorian resolves to reconcile with Sibyl and plead for her forgiveness, only to be informed that a heartbroken Sibyl has taken her own life. Denied an opportunity for redemption, Dorian hides the portrait in a locked room and slips further and further into a life of debauchery and sensual excess.

When published in book form in 1891, Oscar Wilde wrote a preface to the novel that was effectively a manifesto in support of the fin de siècle movement in art and philosophy that attracted Wilde. In this he states, 'There is no such thing as a moral or immoral book. Books are well written or badly written. That is all.' Wilde was responding to criticism of the novel, which had caused much controversy on its original publication in a literary magazine because of its portrayal of hedonism and thinly disguised homoeroticism. In fact, *The Picture of Dorian Gray* is a deeply moral book about the consequences of the pursuit of pleasure without responsibility.

FRANKENSTEIN
BY MARY SHELLEY

SYNOPSIS

A talented and ambitious scientist succeeds in breathing life into an artificial being, hoping his experiments will benefit humanity. However, his creature is a hideously deformed monster and is rejected by its creator and other humans, leading it to seek revenge.

LIFE LESSON

It is dangerous to 'play at being God' without considering the impact and consequences of scientific progress. People need to feel that they belong and have proper human connections in order to survive in life.

Published in 1818 with the full title *Frankenstein, or, The Modern Prometheus*, this is a Gothic novel told from three different perspectives. The beginning section is recounted in letters to his sister from Captain Walton, the leader of an expedition to the North Pole. Walton describes seeing a giant figure driving a dog sled across the ice and some hours later happening upon a man, Victor Frankenstein, who is suffering from the effects of malnutrition and hypothermia.

Frankenstein then takes over the narrative and tells his story, including his scientific experiments up to the point he reanimates his humanoid only to be horrified at the results. He then shuns his monster.

A third embedded narration is taken up by the monster, with his story presumably having been recounted at some point to Victor. The monster tells of his battle to survive in the human world and the fear, rejection and hostility his appearance provokes in people. Eventually the monster, although embittered by Victor's abandonment, decides he must seek out his creator as Frankenstein alone has the responsibility to help him find a way to live. Haunted by the results of his experiments and fearful of the possible consequences for humanity if he creates a mate for the monster, Victor betrays his creation a second time, leading to a trail of murder and a bitter fight to the death.

Although often thought of as a Gothic horror story, *Frankenstein* is also one of the earliest works of science fiction. The book is remarkably ambitious in its complex themes and narrative scope considering Shelley was only nineteen years old when she wrote it.

Did You Know?

The common notion of Frankenstein's monster as a creature made from human body parts which are haphazardly sewn and bolted together and reanimated using electricity is a departure from Shelley's original creation. In the novel Victor discovers a hidden element needed for creating life and spends two years moulding his humanoid figure from animal parts acquired 'from the dissecting room and slaughter-house'. The image of Frankenstein's monster on Halloween masks and in comic books is entirely a creation of Hollywood, dating back to costume designs of the 1931 film adaptation starring Boris Karloff as the creature.

ULYSSES BY JAMES JOYCE

SYNOPSIS

Experimental modernist novel recounting the thoughts, movements and encounters of Leopold Bloom during a single day, 16 June 1904, in Dublin, Ireland.

LIFE LESSON

Human consciousness is a miracle and enables us
to see the extraordinary in ordinary experiences,
making each individual life precious and unique.

Considered to be one of the greatest prose works in history, *Ulysses* concerns one day in the life of Leopold Bloom, the principal character, his wife Molly Bloom and Stephen Dedalus, an acquaintance of Bloom's. Divided into eighteen sections or episodes, each part correlates to characters or incidents in Homer's *Odyssey* (Ulysses is the Latin name for Odysseus, the hero of the *Odyssey*).

In Homer's epic poem, Odysseus encounters storms and shipwrecks, gods and monsters in his quest to return to his wife. Leopold Bloom's much more mundane wanderings around Dublin before returning to his wife are wilfully ironic in their correlations to Homer. For example, Circe, the sorceress who seduces Odysseus and brings him under her spell, is represented by Bella Cohen, a local madam who runs a brothel Bloom and Dedalus visit. The monstrous Cyclops in Homer is satirized in *Ulysses* as a drunken, raging anti-Semite, 'blinded' by his hate-filled nationalist rhetoric, and known only as the Citizen, with whom Bloom has an argument in Barney Kiernan's pub. When Odysseus escapes from the Cyclops, he taunts the creature as he and his men sail away, provoking the monster to hurl a huge rock at the boats. As Bloom escapes from the pub in *Ulysses*, the Citizen throws a biscuit tin at him.

Published in 1922, *Ulysses* is revered by scholars and critics for its innovative and experimental use of language. Joyce deploys not only classical allusions but also constantly plays with words through stream of consciousness, puns, broken syntax and strange punctuation to try to replicate and illuminate the thought processes of the human mind. The narrative structure is often playful, too, with shifting perspectives and voices, strange hallucinations and diversions. Although it does not seem to have any clear moral message or purpose other than an evocation of human consciousness, the characters in *Ulysses* ruminate on and discuss a huge spectrum of subjects including politics, art, history, philosophy and religion.

Ulysses is an extremely difficult book to read and intentionally so, but it is a treasure trove of insights ('History is a nightmare from which I am trying to awake'). It is a phenomenal work of art and an homage to the beguiling power of language.

THE STRANGE CASE OF DR JEKYLL AND MR HYDE BY ROBERT LOUIS STEVENSON

SYNOPSIS

A lawyer investigates a series of strange occurrences relating to his friend Dr Jekyll and the doctor's association with the mysterious Mr Hyde.

LIFE LESSON

The ultimate expression of the duality of human nature and the battle between good and evil and an allegorical analysis of addiction.

Published in 1886, *The Strange Case of Dr Jekyll and Mr Hyde* is a classic Gothic novella which has spawned countless adaptations for the stage and screen. The plot concerns the efforts by Gabriel John Utterson to uncover the truth behind his friend Dr Jekyll's connection to a Mr Hyde and a series of violent events. The narrative is essentially a detective story with Utterson as the detective; although Stevenson uses an omniscient narrator, the reader is told of Utterson's thoughts, suspicions and reflections. The story is later taken up in two confessional letters that reveal that Jekyll and Hyde are the same person, one letter from Jekyll's friend Dr Lanyon and the other from Jekyll himself.

Although often seen as a battle between good and evil, the novel can also be read as an allegory of addiction. Jekyll initially sets out to undertake a scientific experiment, believing if he can separate the dark urges of his alter ego, they can be isolated and eliminated. However, he becomes addicted to the freedom and indulgence that transforming into Hyde affords him, and has to take larger and larger doses to return to normality, echoing a classic cycle of addiction to drugs or alcohol. This is particularly evident in Jekyll's behaviour, withdrawing from people and entering into a state of self-denial and delusion as his dependency on the serum grows. Another thematic aspect of the novel is the disparity between public persona and private actions. Stevenson's story can be viewed as an example of the darker underside of Victorian morality, where sins and vices lurked behind an outward veneer of respectability.

THE IMP OF THE PERVERSE
BY EDGAR ALLAN POE

SYNOPSIS

A short story outlining a murder committed
by a man who manages to conceal his crime
for several years until he is suddenly gripped
by an uncontrollable urge to confess.

LIFE LESSON

The dark side of the human psyche can drive
people to act upon self-destructive impulses.

This short story, published in 1845, uses the essay framework
to examine a psychological dilemma. A man commits a
murder by poisoning another man with a noxious candle
that emits fatal fumes. The murderer inherits the dead man's
estate and his crime goes undetected for many years until
one day the man is gripped by the thought that the only
way his crime would be uncovered would be if he was to
voluntarily confess. The murderer becomes so gripped by
the urge to self-destruct he eventually succumbs to what Poe
describes as 'the imp of the perverse', characterized as a small
demon of the dark side of the psyche that puts damaging
thoughts into our minds. The man confesses to the murder,
and is tried and hanged.

In the story Poe extrapolates on this theory by giving the example of someone standing on a precipice and having a sudden dark urge to jump off:

> 'We stand upon the brink of a precipice. We peer into the abyss—we grow sick and dizzy. Our first impulse is to shrink away from the danger. Unaccountably we remain ... It is merely the idea of what would be our sensations during the sweeping precipitancy of a fall from such a height ... for this very cause do we now the most vividly desire it.'

Some critics have pointed out Poe's own self-destructive behaviour throughout his life, and interpret stories such as *The Imp of the Perverse* and *The Black Cat* as Poe's attempts to analyse and explore his own inner demons.

CHAPTER 5

HISTORY AND MEMORY

This last chapter focuses on representations of key historical events on one hand, and memories and memoirs on the other. The modernist writers Virginia Woolf and William Faulkner explore memory as constructs of human consciousness, noting the tragedy of being unable to recover lost time and the dread of time passing. Vladimir Nabokov, Iris Murdoch and Alice Munro explore the role of memory as a creative process and question the reliability of memories recalled through the prism of time. Orhan Pamuk explores how people imbue objects with memories and how these objects can help to preserve the past.

This section concerns fiction set in a range of real historical periods such as apartheid-era South Africa, the Indian independence movement or the dictatorial regime of Juan Vicente Gómez in early twentieth-century Venezuela. These novels shine a light upon historical epochs and movements and enrich our understanding of their significance through their fictional recreations and evocations.

THE SOUND AND THE FURY
BY WILLIAM FAULKNER

SYNOPSIS

The story of the decline of the Compson family, a once respected Southern aristocratic family, told through the fractured thoughts and memories of three brothers.

LIFE LESSON

Memories are an unbreakable and inescapable link to the past, but time is constantly changing and people cannot live in the past.

Published in 1929, Faulkner's fourth novel is considered to be his masterpiece. It also marks a radical departure in his writing style with its use of stream of consciousness, interior monologues and multiple narrators. The novel is divided into four parts, each given a different narrative voice. The first part is the thoughts and 'memories' of Benjy, one of the Compson brothers, who has a mental disability. As a result of his condition, Benjy's memories are disjointed and non-linear.

The second part is narrated by Quentin, the eldest and most intelligent of the Compson brothers, who is at Harvard University. Quentin's thoughts are also non-linear and reflect his anxiety and neuroses, flitting between memories of Caddy, his estranged sister, his sense of alienation from his father, and his preoccupation with death as a means to escape the present and the past.

The third section, concerning the thoughts and motivations of Jason Compson, has the most linear narration, reflecting perhaps that Jason is uncomplicated in terms of his psychology. Cynical, manipulative and openly racist, Jason has been embezzling money meant as maintenance payments for his niece Miss Quentin, and represents the moral bankruptcy into which the Compson family has fallen.

The final section utilizes an omniscient narrator and centres on Dilsey, the mother of the family of servants in the Compson's employ. A deeply spiritual woman, she remains loyal to the Compson family despite being maltreated and abused. She helps to care for Benjy and takes him to Church.

The Sound and the Fury is not an easy read, particularly the first section narrated by Benjy, which necessarily is disorientating, mirroring the confusion in the narrator's mind. Apart from section two which jumps back in time to the day of Quentin's death, the chronology of the 'action' of the novel symbolically takes place over an Easter weekend (although even this is disrupted, with Jason's section taking place on Good Friday, the day before Benjy's). Beneath Faulkner's tricks with time, consciousness, memory and perception, however, lies a deeply sad book about change and decline, and the impossibility of living in the past.

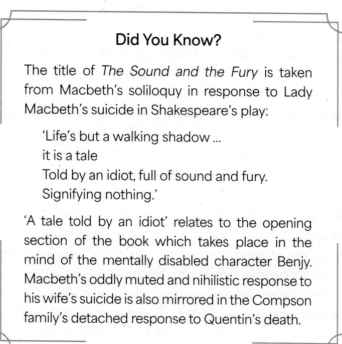

Did You Know?

The title of *The Sound and the Fury* is taken from Macbeth's soliloquy in response to Lady Macbeth's suicide in Shakespeare's play:

'Life's but a walking shadow ...
it is a tale
Told by an idiot, full of sound and fury.
Signifying nothing.'

'A tale told by an idiot' relates to the opening section of the book which takes place in the mind of the mentally disabled character Benjy. Macbeth's oddly muted and nihilistic response to his wife's suicide is also mirrored in the Compson family's detached response to Quentin's death.

THE SEA, THE SEA
BY IRIS MURDOCH

SYNOPSIS

A retired playwright, actor and theatre director
moves to the coast to write his memoirs
and encounters a former lover with whom
he develops an unhealthy obsession.

LIFE LESSON

A meditation on art, the unreliability of
memory, delusion and obsession and the 'truth
of the untruths' we present to the world.

Winning the Booker Prize for 1978, the year it was published, *The Sea, the Sea* is the story of Charles Arrowby, who retires from the theatrical world of London to a cottage by the sea where he plans to live in solitude, eat well and write his memoirs. Vain, arrogant and self-absorbed, Arrowby's delusions, self-deceptions, petty jealousies and obsessions are gradually revealed through a series of encounters with former lovers and associates.

Arrowby is a sociopath, incapable of appreciating or understanding the thoughts and feelings of others, content to idealize his past love with little regard for the actual reality or truth of his relationships and actions in the present. Murdoch uses the memoir form to explore the idea of how memories are always filtered by present experience and can change over time. At the end of the novel, disillusioned by his life in the country, Arrowby returns to London and reflects upon the unreliability or falseness of memories: '... loose ends can never be properly tied, one is always producing new ones. Time, like the sea, unties all knots. Judgments on people are never final, they emerge from summings up which at once suggest the need of a reconsideration.'

The Sea, the Sea presents a fascinating study of a mind teetering on the brink of madness through self-delusion and self-deception. Although in essence a psychological novel, it is darkly comic in places and is densely and beautifully written, particularly the descriptions of the coastline and of course, the sea itself, which takes on a magical and mystical quality.

MRS DALLOWAY
BY VIRGINIA WOOLF

SYNOPSIS

The thoughts, feelings, memories and dreams of an upper-class housewife in post-First World War London spread over a single day as she prepares for and hosts a party.

LIFE LESSON

Living life according to how we perceive society dictates we should, makes us feel unfulfilled and leads to an oppressive sense of loss. It is difficult to adapt to both personal and social change, or make sense of present experience, when the world in general is also rapidly changing.

This stream of consciousness novel covers a day in the life of Clarissa Dalloway, a middle-aged London socialite. Published in 1925, the book has no plot in the conventional sense, but consists of a series of episodes and moments that are described through the thoughts, feelings, memories and dreams of the characters Mrs Dalloway encounters.

Apart from Clarissa, the other principal character is Septimus Smith, a traumatized veteran of the First World War who is suffering from post-traumatic stress disorder. Although Clarissa and Septimus do not meet (they pass each other unwittingly in the street) they act as alter egos or 'doubles' of each other, and are reflected in each other's thoughts. Both feel their individuality has been compromised and oppressed, and regret poor choices in their past: Clarissa marrying Richard due to social and financial expediency, and Septimus enlisting in the army due to misplaced romantic notions of patriotism and heroism. The crushing sense of remorse and the torture of memories have led Clarissa and Septimus into struggles with mental health.

Time and memory are important themes and motifs throughout *Mrs Dalloway*. The chimes of Big Ben intrude at regular intervals, signifying the passing of time that Clarissa so morbidly dreads. This is a complex book and is seen by some critics as a companion novel or answer to James Joyce's *Ulysses*. There is a passing resemblance between the two novels in that they are both set during a single day and show myriad different perspectives. They can also both be seen as modernist works exploring new methods of describing human consciousness.

DOÑA BÁRBARA
BY RÓMULO GALLEGOS

SYNOPSIS
An educated lawyer returns to his family's farm in rural Venezuela to find it has been annexed and is under the control of a tyrannical rival landowner, the femme fatale Doña Bárbara. A power struggle ensues.

LIFE LESSON
Progress and modernity can have a civilizing power.

This 1929 novel by Venezuelan author Rómulo Gallegos recounts the tale of Santos Luzardo, a cultured man who returns to his family's farm on Venezuela's plains only to find his ranch has been stolen from him by Doña Bárbara, an infamous woman with a fearsome reputation. Luzardo initially intended to sell the land but resolves to stay and reclaim the land by civilized, legal means.

The battle of wills between Luzardo and Doña Bárbara is a metaphor for the struggle for the soul of Venezuela's rural wilderness. Santos Luzardo represents the modernizing movement in many parts of South America in the early twentieth century: the urban, educated professional class who wished to civilize the rural populations and raise them above tribal systems or rule by local 'strongmen'. Doña Bárbara, on the other hand, represents the savagery and brutality of the past, a society in which power and violence prevailed in a rule of fear and superstition.

Gallegos's novel can also partly be read as a socio-political allegory of Venezuela. In the 1920s, the country was ruled by the dictator Juan Vicente Gómez. Using the profits from recently discovered oil reserves, Gómez modernized parts of the country, bringing prosperity to a small group of elites. However, his regime was riddled with corruption and brutality, especially towards any opposition figures.

BURGER'S DAUGHTER
BY NADINE GORDIMER

SYNOPSIS

In apartheid-era South Africa, a young Afrikaner woman journeys towards political consciousness and acceptance of her father's legacy as a noted activist who died in captivity.

LIFE LESSON

Human conflict and tension occur when the desire for personal and private identity is challenged by social and political responsibility.

Published in 1979, *Burger's Daughter* begins the story of Rosa Burger in 1970s South Africa. Rosa's parents are famous white South African activists who dedicate their lives to protesting against apartheid and campaigning for equality for black South Africans.

The novel alternates between first person and third person narration and uses flashbacks to Rosa's childhood growing up in a household that was a sanctuary for the poor and politically oppressed. The bulk of the action is set a year after her father's death and concerns Rosa's attempt to initially try to distance herself from her parents' political stance. However, because of who she is and the people she knows (mainly comrades of her parents), she is subject to surveillance by the South African state and is denied a passport. Eventually, through the intervention of a powerful acquaintance, Rosa is able to acquire the papers to visit France and plans to go into exile.

For a while Rosa is able to live her own life and no longer feels the burden of being the daughter of a revered revolutionary. While on holiday in London, however, she attends some political meetings about apartheid and a chance encounter with a childhood friend ignites her dormant political consciousness.

Burgher's Daughter depicts the brutality of the apartheid regime and the efforts to resist it. However, it is also the story of one woman coming to terms with her own identity and sense of moral responsibility.

MIDNIGHT'S CHILDREN
BY SALMAN RUSHDIE

SYNOPSIS

A postmodern, postcolonial novel detailing the intertwined lives of two children born at the same point in history, the first hour of Indian independence from British colonial rule.

LIFE LESSON

A culture that has been under colonial repression for a long time will inevitably struggle to rediscover and reassert its own identity, leading to a great deal of violence and conflict.

The experiences of three generations of the Sinai family in India are related in this 1981 novel set in the years leading up to and after India's independence from British rule. The family's history is recounted by Saleem Sinai, one of the 'midnight's children', those born during the first hour of Indian independence, who are blessed (or in some senses cursed) with magical powers. Saleem works in a pickle factory by day and records his often fantastical tales by night with the help of his loyal companion Padma.

Saleem's 'autobiography' is set against the backdrop of many of the major events of India's turbulent twentieth-century history. Through the prism of his stories a picture emerges of the strife and turmoil of modern India: the divisions and dissents, the tensions between communities and classes, religious fanaticism and the conflict between traditional values and modernizing influences.

In *Midnight's Children* Rushdie deploys various postmodern literary devices such as self-reflexivity or self-reflection by the narrator, which is emphasized by the unreliability of Saleem's memories. At various points in the novel, Saleem makes errors in his recollections, or misremembers historical facts. Saleem initially frets that these errors in his memory may be symptoms of his declining mental health but often declines to correct them, deciding that they are how he recalled events and so represent his own personal truth. Memory in this respect becomes a creative act and allows Saleem the personal liberty to construct his identity, his history and his world.

Midnight's Children is a complex book that crosses genres, mixes fact with fiction, comedy with tragedy, and fantasy with reality to produce an allegorical tale depicting India's journey from colonial rule to independence and partition.

THE MUSEUM OF INNOCENCE
BY ORHAN PAMUK

SYNOPSIS

Set in Istanbul in the 1970s and 1980s, Kemal, a wealthy upper-class businessman who is engaged to be married, falls in love with Füsun, a lowly young shop-girl, and begins a passionate affair. Torn between the expectations of his caste and his all-consuming love for Füsun, Kemal loses the love of his life and sets about reclaiming her by collecting objects redolent of their love for each other.

LIFE LESSON

Memories can be invested in objects as a powerful reminder of things lost through the inexorable passing of time. It is tragically impossible to recreate the past.

The Museum of Innocence (2008) follows a familiar trope of impossible love that is lost through the external pressure of class conventions. However, when his love Füsun disappears after Kemal becomes engaged to the woman his family approve of, he is plunged into a deep well of misery, and the novel takes on a decidedly darker tone. When finally they meet again, although noticeably only on Füsun's terms, Kemal struggles desperately to reignite their former passion. He starts to steal objects from her house in a symbolic attempt to 'reclaim her'.

Pamuk's novel is an unconventional love story, but it is also a philosophical treatise. He explores how to preserve memories and not distort them through time and the rose-tinted hue of hindsight. The historical setting returns to a key theme in Pamuk's fiction, namely the clash between the old, traditional culture of the East and the more modern, commercial and materialistic cultural values of the West. It is a melancholic and tragic love story that covers themes of memory, regret and female identity.

Did You Know?

The museum that Kemal creates at the end of *The Museum of Innocence* actually exists in Istanbul. Pamuk began collecting curiosities while developing the novel. Sometimes an object would inspire a new story within the narrative and on other occasions he would search for items to illustrate existing scenes. The collection was originally intended as an exhibition to mark the novel's publication in 2008, but the museum opened four years later as Pamuk's concept widened. It consists of eighty-three displays corresponding to the eighty-three chapters of the novel, and contains objects described in the story and other ephemera redolent of Istanbul in the 1970s. Visitors can gain free entry to the museum by bringing along a copy of the book, which contains a ticket printed in the final chapter.

THE GREAT INDIAN NOVEL
BY SHASHI THAROOR

SYNOPSIS

Satirical historical novel that transposes the Hindu
epic poem the *Mahabharata* onto a fictional
recounting of modern Indian history from
the Indian independence movement through
to the first decades of postcolonial rule.

LIFE LESSON

'Peace is not the absence of conflict but the
ability to cope with it.' – Mahātmā Gandhi.

The ancient Indian tale of the *Mahabharata* tells the story
of the dynastic conflict over sovereignty of the kingdom
of Hastinapur between the Pandavas and the Kauravas, two
opposing strands of the heirs of King Shantanu. *The Great
Indian Novel*, published in 1989, takes this folk mythology as a
framing device to tell the story of modern Indian history.

The novel's title is a hyperbolic pun alluding to several
things: the 'Great American Novel'; a partial translation
in English of *maha* meaning 'great'; and *Bharata* as an
alternative name for India. Tharoor re-presents the story of the
emerging Indian democratic movement as a conflict between
groups and individuals entangled by their private and political

histories. Characters in his novel are assigned a correlating character from the *Mahabharata*, often satirically. For example, Mahātmā Gandhi is aligned with the character of Bhishma, the celibate son of King Shantanu (Gandhi was an advocate of celibacy), and Dhritarashtra, the blind king of Hastinapur in the epic, is represented by the Indian nationalist politician Jawaharlal Nehru, who had the nickname 'the blind idealist'.

Tharoor mixes parody, irony, allusion and wordplay to create a narrative as complex and tangled as its historical subject matter. In the spirit of true satire, he turns his eye on many aspects of modern Indian history and culture, including what were previously considered to be 'sacred cows', such as his irreverent and sarcastic depiction of Gandhi. Although familiarity with the *Mahabharata* and modern Indian politics is no doubt advantageous when reading *The Great Indian Novel*, there are rewards to be had from researching the targets of Tharoor's ridicule in this clever, funny and informative work.

PALE FIRE BY
VLADIMIR NABOKOV

SYNOPSIS

A novel in the form of a 999-line poem with accompanying foreword, commentary and index providing the framing structure for an experimental treatise about memory, madness and death.

LIFE LESSON

Memories are ordered in the mind by narrative
structures and are artistic constructs, this can
lead them to be unreliable and illusory.

This is an extraordinary work which pre-figures and anticipates
the postmodern novel and modern metafiction. Published in
1962, the 'novel' (and Nabokov would no doubt approve of
the quotation marks as he once wryly remarked that the word
'reality' should always be written inside inverted commas) is
embedded in footnotes that form a critical commentary on an
epic poem written in heroic couplets.

An aging, respected American poet, John Shade, has been
killed after (nearly) completing a major work which reflects
upon the tragedies and losses in his life and contemplates,
philosophically, the nature of death. This poem, however, has
been hijacked by a fellow academic, Charles Kinbote, who has
an entirely different story to tell. Kinbote may, or may not,
be insane.

Nabokov's masterpiece is a multi-dimensional work which
wilfully defies categorization. The 999-line poem is a pitch-
perfect parody of Alexander Pope's mastery of poetic form
mixed with Robert Frost's pastoral and confessional tone,
and has at its centre the sad story of John Shade's daughter's
suicide.

Kinbote's wild, delusional commentary is funny, sad and
dark in equal measure, filled with clever allusions, tricks,
deliberate deceptions, missteps and sly jokes, which the
casual reader may blink and miss. One example is when
Shade, describing objects in the bedroom of his dead aunt,

mentions a newspaper article describing a baseball home run, 'Chapman's Homer'. Kinbote's commentary is that the printer has mistakenly put in the title of John Keats' sonnet 'On First Looking into Chapman's Homer'.

The fact that Kinbote fails to acknowledge or understand the joke opens up a question about interpretation and meaning in art. Yet the choice of the Keats' reference itself cannot be arbitrary, as the sonnet in question is an ode to the power and wonderment that art instils in the human soul, a profound thrill that reading a novel as bewilderingly brilliant as *Pale Fire* also provokes.

SPRING SNOW
BY YUKIO MISHIMA

SYNOPSIS

Tragic Japanese love story about the doomed romance between Kiyoaki Matsugae, the son of an upwardly mobile family, and Satoko Ayakura, the beautiful daughter of a fading aristocratic family.

LIFE LESSON

New values of modernization and progress clash with the dying cultures and traditions of the past.

The first in a series of novels known as *The Sea of Fertility* tetralogy, *Spring Snow* was published in 1969 and is set in

Tokyo in 1912, at a time of social upheaval and cultural transition. The story centres on Kiyoaki, a sensitive young man from Japan's emergent middle class, who falls in love with Satoko, a girl from a very traditional aristocratic family. Custom demands that Satoko's family arrange a marriage for her and that she should undergo a traditional ritual of courtship and betrothal. So, an arrangement is made for Satoko to be engaged to marry Prince Harunori Toin, from another traditional imperial court family. Having previously been in a state of confused denial and fear over his intense feelings for Satoko, news of the engagement sparks in Kiyoko the realization that Satoko is his true love, and the pair begin a torrid and doomed illicit affair.

Set in a period when Japan was emerging from feudal isolation and feeling the impact of Westernization on its cultural values, *Spring Snow* explores the conflict between private and public lives and the friction between past and present. The novel also examines individuals who are enslaved and tormented by their emotions and are confined by the social strictures and customs to which they adhere. It is a melancholy, existential drama with vibrant poetry, adorned with vivid symbolism from nature and much philosophy on the meaning of existence and the essence of love and death.

THE REMAINS OF THE DAY
BY KAZUO ISHIGURO

SYNOPSIS

An aging butler in an English stately home receives a letter from a former colleague and sets off on a road trip during which he reminisces about his life in service.

LIFE LESSON

Denial and suppression of true feelings and emotions leads to regrets about missed opportunities and false steps.

This novel, published in 1989, is told through the diary entries of Stevens, an elderly, long-serving butler at Darlington Hall, an English country house. Stevens unexpectedly receives a letter from Miss Kenton, a former colleague, which brings back long-dormant feelings. Darlington Hall is in danger of being sold and is in need of a housekeeper, and Stevens is encouraged by his American employer to take a short vacation and visit his former friend to try to entice her to return to her former position.

As Stevens drives through the English countryside, he reminisces about his life and his relationships with three people: his father; Lord Darlington, his long-standing previous employer; and Miss Kenton.

Stevens served Lord Darlington devotedly for many years and through his recollections it is revealed that his former employer was a Nazi sympathizer in the lead-up to the Second World War. Although Stevens remained steadfastly loyal to his employer (he had previously believed Lord Darlington to be a great and dignified man), he becomes concerned that perhaps he was mistaken as to the true nature of his employer's character.

As Stevens nears his destination, more details and thoughts emerge concerning his relationship with Miss Kenyon, and it seems that a mutual attraction and love for each other might have been suppressed in the name of professional duty. There were times when the couple could have acted upon their feelings, but Stevens's reticence and subservience to his role left their relationship unfulfilled – a missed opportunity that Stevens now recognizes and deeply regrets.

In *The Remains of the Day*, Ishiguro paints a touching and sad portrait of a man devoting his life to a notion of service and duty. He also describes a class system that instils a stifling hierarchy upon people, thwarting their chances of happiness and self-fulfilment.

ON THE ROAD
BY JACK KEROUAC

SYNOPSIS

Autobiographical novel detailing a series of wild
road trips across America undertaken in the
late 1940s in search of consciousness-altering
experiences and freedom from conformity.

LIFE LESSON

It is important to be able to live in the moment
and to embrace spontaneity as part of a journey
towards spiritual self-awareness and freedom.

On the Road (1957) tells the story of several journeys across
America made by the narrator and author, Sal Paradise, and his
friends, most notably the free-living maverick Dean Moriarty.
Along the way the two men have love affairs, attend parties,
take on short-term, dead-end jobs, take drugs and listen to
jazz. They listen to a lot of jazz …

The novel became a manifesto for the early post-war
counterculture of what Kerouac himself termed the 'Beat
Generation', and is perhaps best viewed as a memoir of that
particular era of American cultural history. The generation
Kerouac describes had lived through the Great Depression and
the Second World War, and many of its members were eager

to break off the shackles of conventional society and seek out alternative ways to find fulfilment through lived experiences.

Kerouac deploys stream of consciousness techniques, and modelled much of his prose style along the lines of the spontaneous and improvisational methods of jazz musicians by experimenting with the sounds of words and the use of punctuation marks. Kerouac also famously was opposed to editing his work, believing the words written down were born from the purity of inspiration and that rewriting constituted a form of 'self-censorship'.

On the Road, for all of its reputation as a counterculture bible or manifesto for alternative living, is at its heart a book about the enduring power of friendship, and the emotional and spiritual pleasures gleaned from having the freedom to travel and share experiences.

Did You Know?

The manuscript was composed by Kerouac on a 120-feet-long continuous scroll of pages of tracing paper cut to fit into a typewriter and then taped together. Kerouac typed it up in twenty days during April 1951 during which period he barely slept and existed solely on coffee, Benzedrine and pea soup. The scroll was sold at auction in 2001 for $2.43 million to a businessman, and has been exhibited in museums and libraries in the USA, the UK and France.

THE BOOK OF LAUGHTER AND FORGETTING BY MILAN KUNDERA

SYNOPSIS

A novel composed of seven separate but related narratives concerning the lives of Czech citizens living in Prague or in exile in the aftermath of the Soviet invasion of 1968.

LIFE LESSON

Totalitarian regimes alter history and rewrite or erase memories. People, on a personal and emotional level, choose whether to recall or forget memories.

Written by the Czech author while he was in exile in France in the late 1970s and published in 1979, this novel combines seven narratives around the theme of memories. The book is not, however, a conventional short story collection, as each section has a consistent authorial voice who regularly interjects to make observations or meditate on particular philosophical questions relating to memory, the nature and source of laughter, the human capacity for self-preservation and the experience of living in exile.

The thematic cross-referencing between the separate stories can be oblique but is also quite often suggested clearly. Sections one and four, for example, share the same title of 'Lost Letters' and concern two characters searching for written documents, but for polarising reasons. In section one, Mirek is trying to retrieve love letters so he can either alter or destroy a memory/history; in section four Tamina, living in exile, is trying to retrieve letters so she may preserve her memories of her dead husband. The novel also contains elements of magic realism, such as one section with a meeting of dead poets: Voltaire, Lermontov, Goethe and Petrarch, which is an ironic joke about the preservation of history and creative impulses. *The Book of Laughter and Forgetting* is a philosophical treatise on memory, both personal and historical, and how vital it is to preserve memories, particularly in the face of totalitarian oppression.

WHAT IS REMEMBERED
BY ALICE MUNRO

SYNOPSIS

A widow recalls the circumstances of a fleeting affair she had thirty years previously and rediscovers a seemingly significant detail.

LIFE LESSON

What we choose to remember and what we choose to forget shows how mysterious human memory is.

This is a short story by a Canadian Nobel Prize-winning author which was published in Munro's 2001 collection: *Hateship, Friendship, Courtship, Loveship, Marriage*.

Meriel, an elderly widow, recalls through flashback an incident from her past when she was in her late twenties. While attending the funeral of her husband Pierre's best friend, Meriel meets a young doctor. The funeral is near the home of Meriel's old family friend (called Muriel and Meriel's namesake) and Meriel decides to visit her. The doctor offers to drive Meriel and the two of them have a brief sexual tryst. The affair, as such, only occurred during the course of a single day and Meriel never had any contact with the doctor again, and yet her memory of the day remains vivid.

As Meriel pores over her recollections she starts to reimagine moments she spent with the doctor/lover and begins to create in her mind a parallel narrative, changing settings, scenes and details, and speculating as to how different her life may have been. Ultimately, it is this escape into her reimagining that is important for Meriel's sense of self. Although it was just a fleeting moment in her life, the act of remembering this moment which made her feel alive is what she seeks to preserve: 'The job she had to do, as she saw it, was to remember everything – and by "remember" she meant experience it in her mind, one more time – then store it away forever.'

INDEX OF AUTHORS

Achebe, Chinua 89
Adams, Richard 1
Amado, Jorge 40
Armah, Ayi Kwei 111
Atwood, Margaret 106
Austen, Jane 16

Baldwin, James 84
Bellow, Saul 138
Borges, Jorge Luis 121
Bovary, Madame 9
Brontë, Charlotte 8
Brontë, Emily 17
Bulgakov, Mikhail 98
Burgess, Anthony 51

Camus, Albert 132
Carver, Raymond 86
Cervantes, Miguel de 124
Chekov, Anton 32
Coetzee, J.M. 103
Conrad, Joseph 108

Dazai, Osamu 134
Dickens, Charles 36, 71
Dostoevsky, Fyodor 144

Eliot, George 54
Ellison, Ralph 91

Faulkner, William 158
Fitzgerald, F. Scott 58
Flaubert, Gustav 9
Ford, Madox Ford 28
Forster, E.M. 31

Gallegos, Rómulo 164
Goethe, Johann Wolfgang von 20
Gogol, Nikolai 38

Golding, William 76
Goncharov, Ivan 128
Gordimer, Nadine 165
Grass, Günter 104
Greene, Graham 126

Hamsun, Knut 141
Hardy, Thomas 26
Hašek, Jaroslav 113
Heller, Joseph 109
Heliodorus of Emesa 7
Hemingway, Ernest 68
Hugo, Victor 70
Huxley, Aldous 118

Ishiguro, Kazuo 176

James, Henry 75
Joyce, James 151

Kafka, Franz 67
Kerouac, Jack 178
Kesey, Ken 101
Kundera, Milan 180

Laclos, Pierre Choderlos de 23
Lawrence, D.H. 24
Lee, Harper 80
Lermontov, Mikhail 47
Levi, Primo 96
Lu Xun 44

Mann, Thomas 63
Marquez, Gabriel Garcia 12
Mishima, Yukio 174
Morrison, Toni 100
Munro, Alice 181
Murakami, Haruki 146
Murdoch, Iris 160

Nabokov, Vladimir 14, 172

O'Connor, Flannery 78
Orwell, George 48

Pamuk, Orhan 168
Plath, Sylvia 130
Poe, Edgar Allan 155
Pynchon, Thomas 117

Rabelais, François 65
Richardson, Samuel 142
Roth, Philip 73
Roy, Arundhati 29
Rushdie, Salman 167

Salinger, J.D. 139
Shelley, Mary 149
Sōseki, Natsume 42
Spark, Muriel 52
Steinbeck, John 59
Sterne, Laurence 136
Stevenson, Robert Louis 153
Swift, Jonathan 81

Thackeray, William Make-peace 61
Tharoor, Shashi 171
Tolstoy, Leo 19
Twain, Mark 55

Vonnegut, Kurt 94

Walker, Alice 120
Waugh, Evelyn 43
Wilde, Oscar 147
Wolfe, Tom 83
Woolf, Virginia 162

Zola, Emile 114

INDEX OF WORKS

1984 48

Adventures of Augie March, The 138
Adventures of Huckleberry Finn, The 55
Aethiopica 7
American Pastoral 73
Anna Karenina 19

Beautyful Ones Are Not Yet Born, The 111
Bell Jar, The 130
Beloved 100
Bonfire of the Vanities, The 83
Book of Laughter and Forgetting, The 180
Brave New World 118
Burger's Daughter 165

Captain of the Sands 40
Catch-22 109
Catcher in the Rye, The 139
Clockwork Orange, A 51
Color Purple, The 120
Crime and Punishment 144

David Copperfield 36
Dead Souls 38
Diary of a Madman 44
Don Quixote 124
Doña Bárbara 164

Frankenstein 149

Gargantua and Pantagruel 65
Germinal 114
Go Tell It on the Mountain 84
God of Small Things, The 29
Good Soldier, The 28
Good Soldier Švejk, The 113
Gravity's Rainbow 117
Great Expectations 71
Great Gatsby, The 58

Great Indian Novel, The 171
Gulliver's Travels 81

Handful of Dust, A 43
Handmaid's Tale, The 106
Hateship, Friendship, Courtship, Loveship, Marriage 182
Hear the Wind Sing 146
Heart of Darkness 108
Heart of the Matter, The 126
Hero of Our Time, A 47
Hunger 141

I Am a Cat 42
If This is a Man 96
Imp of the Perverse, The 155
Invisible Man 91

Jane Eyre 8

Lady with the Dog, The 32
L'Etranger 132
Les Liaisons Dangereuses 23
Les Misérables 70
Life & Times of Michael K 103
Lolita 14
Lord of the Flies, The 76
Lottery in Babylon, The 121
Love in the Time of Cholera 12

Madame Bovary 9
Magic Mountain, The 63
Master and Margarita, The 98
Metamorphosis 67
Middlemarch 54
Midnight's Children 167
Mrs Dalloway 162
Museum of Innocence, The 168

No Longer Human 134

Oblomov 128
Of Mice and Men 59
Old Man and the Sea, The 68
On the Road 178
One Flew Over the Cuckoo's Nest 101

Pale Fire 172
Pamela 142
Picture of Dorian Gray, The 147
Pinball 146
Portrait of a Lady, The 75
Pride and Prejudice 16
Prime of Miss Jean Brodie, The 52

Remains of the Day, The 176
Room With a View, A 31

Slaughterhouse-Five 94
Small, Good Thing, A 86
Sorrows of Young Werther, The 20
Sound and the Fury, The 158
Spring Snow 174
Strange Case of Dr Jekyll and Mr Hyde, The 153

Tess of the d'Urbervilles 26
The Sea, The Sea 160
Things Fall Apart 89
Tin Drum, The 104
To Kill a Mockingbird 80
Tristram Shandy 136

Ulysses 151

Vanity Fair 61

Watership Down 1–2
What Is Remembered 181
Wild Sheep Chase, A 146
Wise Blood 78
Women in Love 24
Wuthering Heights 17